CW00954338

Edinburgh International Festival 1962

"The Novel Today"

20th-24th August

programme and notes

International Writers' Conference

McEwan Hall, Edinburgh

Kennedy & Boyd
an imprint of
Zeticula Ltd
The Roan
Kilkerran
KA19 8LS
Scotland.

http://www.kennedyandboyd.co.uk
admin@kennedyandboyd.co.uk

First published in 1962.
This edition is limited to 150 signed copies, of which this is number   121

Copyright © Zeticula 2012.

ISBN 978-1-84921-073-7

writers
and
critics

Chief Editor   A. NORMAN JEFFARES
Advisory Editors   DAVID DAICHES
                    C. P. SNOW

Paperback
Price 5s. 0d. each

1   **EZRA POUND** G. S. Fraser
2   **HENRY JAMES** D. W. Jefferson
3   **ROBERT GRAVES** J. M. Cohen
4   **WALLACE STEVENS** Frank Kermode
5   **IONESCO** Richard N. Coe
6   **FAULKNER** Michael Millgate
7   **HEMINGWAY** Stewart Sanderson
8   **BRECHT** Ronald Gray
9   **COLETTE** Margaret Davies
10   **D. H. LAWRENCE** Anthony Beal
11   **ARTHUR MILLER** Dennis Welland
12   **WHITMAN** Geoffrey Dutton
13   **E. M. FORSTER** K. W. Gransden
14   **MELVILLE** A. R. Humphreys
15   **SARTRE** Maurice Cranston
16   **STEINBECK** F. W. Watt

OLIVER & BOYD
Tweeddale Court, 14 High Street, Edinburgh 1

Edinburgh University Press

EDINBURGH BOOKS: INTERNATIONAL

in outlook

Independent
AFRICAN
G. A. Shepperson and T. Price
Medium octavo 570 pp. 50s. net
'It is my careful judgment that this is
one of the greatest books on Africa'
Professor Max Gluckman

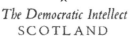

The Democratic Intellect
SCOTLAND
and her Universities in the 19th Century
G. E. Davie
Medium octavo 350 pp. 50s. net
'This admirable book'
Sir Charles Snow in the New Statesman

★

HUNGARY
A Short History
C. A. Macartney
Demy octavo 280 pp. 21s. net
*A new and brilliant survey by the
world's greatest authority on Hungary*

Three Centuries of
FRENCH
Verse
Alan J. Steele
Large crown octavo 350 pp. 21s. net
'Within the historical limits it sets itself, it is probably
the most complete and delightful anthology of
French verse ever compounded'
Modern Language Notes

ISLAM
and the West
Norman Daniel
Medium octavo 450 pp. 63s. net
'M. Daniel fait preuve d'une grande compréhension et
d'une vraie sympathie à l'égard de l'Islam ... On louera la
méthode prudente de l'auteur et ses analyses minutieuses,
soutenues par une erudition très ample'
G. Vajda in Revue de l'histoire des religions

★

Historical Ballads of
DENMARK
Sir Alexander Gray
Royal octavo 168 pp. 30s. net
'An experiment which is triumphantly successful'
Ruari McLean in Connoisseur

Letters from
GOETHE
M. von Herzfeld and C. A. M. Sym
Medium octavo 610 pp. 42s. net
'A boon to readers ... it comprises the fullest and most
responsible selection in English of Goethe's correspondence'
N. Y. Times Book Review

Documentary History of
AMERICAN
Economic Policy since 1789
William Letwin
Demy octavo 436 pp. 40s. net
*A fascinating compilation by an economist at the famous
Massachusetts Institute of Technology*

BYZANTINE
Art
D. Talbot Rice
Crown octavo 93 pp. 12s. 6d. net
'Quest' opera è un brillante lavoro di ricerca'
Rivista Bibliografica

★

A Plea for
MAN
Mario M. Rossi
Large crown octavo 167 pp. 9s. 6d.
'The complement to this historical writing will be found in
great literature: Augustine, Dante, Pascal, the Bible'
The Scotsman

EDINBURGH AUTHORS: INTERNATIONAL

in repute

Edinburgh
International
Festival 1962

"The Novel
Today"

20th-24th August   programme & notes

International
Writers'
Conference

McEwan Hall, Edinburgh

contents

the first literary festival   7

JOHN CALDER

part one: five themes   9

WEIGHTMAN, BRADBURY, DAICHES, CRAIG,
KEIR, MORGAN, WILLIAMS, ROBBE-GRILLET,
MACDONALD, HOOK, DONOGHUE, MACINNES,
WILSON, SARRAUTE, AMIS, TOYNBEE,
NICOLSON, MITCHELL, GUNN, BRAINE,
SPARK

part two: programme and biographical notes   65

part three: survey of contemporary fiction   81

SHEPPERSON, JENKINS, ALLEN,
GEORGE, SINGH, SPEIGHT, HINGLEY,
LOPEZ, MILLGATE, WILLIAMSON

INDEX TO ADVERTISERS   128

international writers' conference

Organisers   John Calder, Sonia Brownell, James Haynes
Artistic Producer   Malcolm Muggeridge

"THE NOVEL TODAY"
Editor   Andrew Hook

Assistant Editor   Kenneth Murcott
Designer   John Martin
Linocuts   Walter Miller

Printer   R & R Clark Ltd, EDINBURGH

address of welcome

from Sir Compton Mackenzie

To my great regret I am unable to
welcome in person the gathering of distinguished
writers from all over the world
who will be meeting in Edinburgh this August.
I venture to think that I speak for every
Scottish author when I say how proud we all are
that so many of our *confrères*
have accepted Edinburgh's invitation
to contribute to the success of
our annual festival.
Fàilte do 'n dùthaich!
Welcome to the country!

THE SCOTSMAN

I N T E R N A T I O N A L

BOOK JACKET EXHIBITION

Adam House, Chambers Street, Edinburgh

A unique collection of books from the leading publishing houses of the world—of absorbing interest to the art designer and book-lover. Over 1,000 books are on display. They range from lavishly illustrated limited editions to paperbacks. They cover every type of book from studies in religion and philosophy to children's books.

Official opening 12 noon, Saturday, AUGUST 18 then open daily from 10 a.m. to 8 p.m. until SEPT. 8, Sundays 2 p.m. to 6 p.m.

ADMISSION FREE

the first literary festival

by JOHN CALDER

Writers' conferences are not new—writers meet fairly frequently under the aegis of such bodies as the International P.E.N.—but usually they meet in private and the outside world knows little of their discussions. The Edinburgh Festival is to be congratulated on sponsoring what is probably the first large-scale conference to be made open to the public, and not only are they providing festival visitors and the citizens of Edinburgh with a new attraction, one very much in keeping with the literary past of the city, but they are doing a great service to contemporary literature in general, and, it is hoped, to Scottish literature in particular. Those coming include not only some of the most eminent and original thinkers of today, but also writers whose reputations are yet to be established outside their own country. The public will have the opportunity of hearing the views of novelists they have read or would like to have read, and they will also learn of the activities of new writers and see how writers themselves are reacting to the great technical revolution taking place in the French novel as a result of the influence of such post-Joyceans as Samuel Beckett and the younger practitioners of the 'new novel'. But although the *avant-garde* looks principally to Paris, many of the new techniques are taking root in such countries as Germany, Poland, Yugoslavia, and Italy, while the United States has an *avant-garde* of its own in the 'beat' novelists and poets, originally centred in San Francisco but now dispersed, whose novels take both their vocabulary and their mystique from the twilight world of jazz and drug-addiction. The American 'beat' and 'hipster' novels already have European imitators, and are probably better known in Great Britain than the French 'new' novels, although many of the more outstanding examples of the former are still not publishable here under the existing obscenity and libel laws. Yet neither school has had a significant influence on British writing, which has changed little since the war, although many distinguished new British novelists have emerged. Many British writers feel that continental trends emphasise novelty for its own sake and that many of the new writers will not last. And yet, when writers meet, it is surprising to see how often they find themselves in agreement. Words like *commitment*, *style*, *reality*, *realism*, *coherence* can take on different meanings for different authors, and very often novelists working in different literary traditions, whose work might seem to be poles apart in style and subject matter, find that they are basically working towards the same objective.

So it is hoped that this first literary festival will do something towards clearing up misunderstandings between intellectuals coming from different countries and literary disciplines and help them to find a common language, and that the interested public will have a unique opportunity to see where novelists differ in their approach and to some extent judge to what extent many of them have succeeded in attaining their objective. In five debates, the discussion will range from a consideration of the relative importance of style, which in the opinion of some of those coming is the first consideration of the novelist as it *dictates* both the subject matter and the reality of the novel (most British novelists would probably take an opposite view), and content—which is not only *plot*, but, among other things, the author's attitude to the moral, social, and political culture in which we live—to, on the last day, a consideration of the future of the novel as entertainment and as an art form. Two of the days inbetween will be devoted to the very controversial topics of *commitment*, the desirability or otherwise of the writer tying himself to the age in which he lives by using his writings as a platform to expose the evils of the day or to further his political, religious, or moral views, and of *censorship*, those restraints whether self-imposed or imposed on the writer from outside, which restrict what he can write and what he can publish. One day, the second, is being devoted entirely to an examination of the Scottish literary scene, and novelists, poets, dramatists, and critics will be participating. It is a happy chance that Hugh MacDiarmid, the outstanding Scottish poet of today, will be taking part during the celebrations connected with his seventieth birthday.

At a time when the advent or increasing popularity of other forms of entertainment, such as television, the theatre, films, and music, have tended to take people increasingly away from the book habit, the importance of any public activity that can awaken interest in what novelists, who are usually among the leading figures in the history of their time, are trying to do, must not be underestimated. If the conference is successful the idea will bear fruit elsewhere and literary festivals may become frequent and widespread. This would have certain concrete results: first of all, writers of talent, who are often among the worst rewarded members of the community, would have an opportunity of reaching the public through personal appearances at conferences, making it easier to establish a reputation than at present, and it would allow them to reap the benefits of cross-fertilisation with the ideas of their counterparts from other countries and of maturer established writers; secondly, literature will travel faster—writers will become known outside their own country sooner than at present (evidence of this is already at hand in reports of the Formentor Conference, which is not open to the public); thirdly, writers will have a platform from which to answer back their critics. Certainly free and open discussion between intellectuals can only contribute positively to the contemporary world, by forging bonds of understanding and, we hope, friendship, between nations. The more that ideas and books are free to travel across national boundaries, the better place the world will be to live in.

The problems of organising the conference have been great. We have had no precedent to guide us, and writers are known to be among the most individualistic, and in some cases temperamental, people in the world. The list of novelists coming has had to be revised up to the very last moment, and even so, the printed list will inevitably contain the names of some writers not present, whereas all those eventually taking part will not necessarily be on the list. There are many reasons for this, other than acts of God. One is that many writers are being sent by their local Writers' Association or by their government or other patron, and it will not be possible to advise us in time of the name of every writer who is being sent. Another is that, writers being writers, many who promised to come will change their minds, and others who could not give us a definite answer in time will turn up after all.

Malcolm Muggeridge will act as Artistic Producer and has planned the form the discussions will take. The technical problems of conducting discussions based on two principal languages, English and French, in such a way that novelists more fluent in other languages can get their points over and be understood by all, are formidable, but we think that the way the discussions are planned and the choice of speakers for each topic should guarantee five fascinating days to the audience. The public are also invited to take part during the final part of each afternoon, and are allowed to put questions either to the chairman for that day, or to individual writers.

So here it is, a Writers' Festival! At the time of writing, we cannot predict even approximately how it will all turn out, but the raw material available is the most lively and stimulating that could be assembled. The conference is an experiment in bringing writers to the public and the public into direct contact with ideas in collision. The audience will learn a great deal, and few will not find their horizons radically widened. But most of all, it should be tremendously exciting, both for those taking part and for those who have come to watch and listen.

part one: *five themes*:

a day-by-day introduction to the topics the conference will discuss

DAY ONE: contrasts of approach

Editorial, page 11
The Variety of the Novel *J G Weightman* page 13
Two Kinds of Novel *Malcolm Bradbury* page 17

DAY TWO: scottish writing today

Editorial, page 21
The Scottish Literary Tradition *David Daiches* page 23
Scottish Literature this Century *David M Craig* page 27
Hugh MacDiarmid *W A S Keir* page 31
The Young Writer in Scotland *Edwin Morgan* page 35

DAY THREE: commitment

Editorial, page 39
Commitment *Raymond Williams* page 41
The Writer's only Commitment is to Literature
Alain Robbe-Grillet page 43
A note from Dwight Macdonald page 44
Commitment & Reality *A D Hook* page 45

DAY FOUR: censorship

Editorial, page 49
Eight Propositions on Censorship *Denis Donoghue* page 51
On Censorship *Colin MacInnes* page 55

DAY FIVE: the novel and the future

Editorial, page 57
Symposium, page 60

Heinemann

Mary McCarthy	On The Contrary	30s
	Stones of Florence *Illustrated*	4 gns
	Memories of a Catholic Girlhood	7s 6d
	A Source of Embarrassment	7s 6d
	Sights and Spectacles	18s
	Venice Observed	15s
Henry Miller	The Air Conditioned Nightmare	30s
	The Colossus of Maroussi	18s
	The Best of Henry Miller	30s
	Edited by Laurence Durrell	
Robert Jungk	Children of the Ashes	25s
Alexander Trocchi	Young Adam	12s 6d
J. B. Priestley	Literature and Western Man	42s
	Thoughts in the Wilderness	21s
	Delight	10s 6d
Truman Capote	The Muses are Heard	6s

Heinemann

day one : contrasts of approach

On its First Day the Conference will discuss the differing approaches to the novel now evident in England and America on the one hand, in France and elsewhere in Europe on the other. Of course in one sense there are as many approaches to the novel as there are novelists; but it is also true that one may recognise the recurring patterns which establish a 'trend'. In the two articles which follow, J G Weightman writes of the inevitability of a variety of approaches to the novel, making particular reference to the French novel, while Malcolm Bradbury describes what he sees as the dominant trends in contemporary English and American fiction.

EYRE &
SPOTTISWOODE

Patrick White

THE LIVING
AND THE DEAD

This is Patrick White's second novel,
written just before 'The Aunt's Story'
and now republished after being long
out of print. It is the only one of his
books set in London and will be of
great interest to the many readers
who find him one of the great literary
figures of our day. *November*, 22s 6d

John Braine

LIFE AT THE TOP

John Braine's new novel picks up the
story of Joe Lampton ten years after
his marriage, enlarging and deepen-
ing the characters of 'Room at the
Top'. In it is all the force and narrative power of the earlier book, allied
to a new tenderness and maturity. It
will add to its author's high reputation. *October*, 18s

the variety of the novel

by J G WEIGHTMAN

J G Weightman is a Lecturer in French at King's College, London, and also a critic and broadcaster.

It is not surprising that there should be so many conflicting views on the novel because, for more than two hundred years now, the word 'novel' has been applied to very different kinds of writing.

Most of us, I suppose, feel vaguely that we can define a 'novel'; it is a longish story, which shows a number of characters linked together by a plot and living through a phase of life, or perhaps even a whole lifetime. Then, if we think back to the last novels we read—*Lady Chatterley's Lover*, say, or *Lolita*—it will probably strike us that, more often than not, the phase of life the novel deals with is the process of falling in or out of love. Most novels are, in the first place, love-stories. This is not simply because love is generally admitted to be an important feature of human experience. If European novels were our only guide to the behaviour of the human race, we should have to conclude that love is by far the *most* important thing in life. The reason is that the novel grew, to some extent, out of the medieval romance, which took as its basic principle the belief in the supreme value of love, invented by the troubadours. Not all novelists have subscribed to this belief. A minority have even struggled to redress the balance by writing novels from which love is entirely excluded, and they have usually tried to do this by emphasising the other strains which fed the novel as it gradually came into being as a definite *genre*.

These strains were, briefly: the epic, which depicted the collective adventure of a group or a nation, usually involved in a war; the pastoral, which created a Utopian dream-world; the picaresque tale which recounted the wanderings of some social misfit; anecdotal memoirs about political or social intrigue; collections of scandalous anecdotes about sexual and other misdemeanours; the fable, which told a story to point a moral; and the fairy-tale, which represented the spontaneous generation in folklore of pre-psychoanalytical imagery.

Almost all novels show a combination of the love-theme with one or more of these strains. *Lady Chatterley's Lover*, for instance, is both love-story and pastoral moral fable, while *Lolita* is a scandalous anecdote raised to the level of passion and treated with picaresque variations and occasional excursions into fantasy.

Arguments about novel-writing between novelists and critics normally arise from differences of opinion about the degree to which some particular strain should be developed, because each strain tends, of course, to have its own underlying philosophy and to call for its particular techniques. Indeed, it is quite common for literary controversies to be based on conflicting preferences for different kinds of novels, instead of being focussed on the success or failure of an individual work within a given kind. For example, people with epic tastes have been known to object to Jane Austen because, instead of giving a general picture of England in the Napoleonic era, she concentrated on love-stories in the form of anecdotal memoirs. Conversely, some of Zola's contemporaries with a liking for refined and intimate psychological studies dubbed him a 'house painter', because he was mainly interested in attempting to portray modern society in vast, panoramic descriptions.

But even when argument is not complicated by misunderstanding, it still remains true that the novel is such a rich and varied form that different novelists often appear to live in different worlds, with little or no communication between them. William Faulkner and Kingsley Amis, Jean-Paul Sartre and Ivy Compton-Burnett, Alain Robbe-Grillet and J. D. Salinger—to mention only six living writers—are so remote from each other that it seems almost impossible, at first sight, to say anything about the novel that is relevant to them all.

On reflection, however, we can perhaps discover certain cross-references. Faulkner and Sartre (at least the Sartre of *Roads to Freedom*) attempt to describe a wide range of people in an epic perspective, and to suggest some sort of moral through their descriptions; that is, they are continuing the panoramic tradition with moral overtones, as it was practised by Balzac, Dickens, Zola, and many others. It just so happens that Faulkner deals with the decayed feudalism of the American Deep South, in semi-biblical language, whereas Sartre writes about a cross-section of French society, in Marxist-Existentialist terms. Amis in *Lucky Jim* and Salinger in *The Catcher in the Rye* exploit what is ultimately a version of the picaresque form; they show a particular society through the eyes of a misfit, who is looking for genuine experience. One hero is a lower-middle-class Englishman trying half-heartedly to make good and get women, while the other is a rich and neurotic young American, whose only function is to be a wryly innocent contemplative. Compton-Burnett and Salinger are similar in that they rely largely for their effects on the rhythms of spoken speech, although one operates in very stylised Edwardian English, while the other uses the most recent American slang. Robbe-Grillet is like Faulkner in that he jumbles his time-sequence, and like Compton-Burnett in that he pays great attention to his formal pattern and uses rhythms and repetitions as important elements in that pattern.

To discover how alike, or unlike, novelists are (independently of their different national backgrounds) we can in fact apply a great many tests, some connected with content, others with technique. We can ask if the author is a Christian or a non-Christian; if he confines himself to the description of one social class or is interested in showing different classes in juxtaposition; if he is only concerned with people as private individuals or also tries to describe them in their professional or political capacities; if he tells the story from one angle or from several; if his tone is predominantly tragic or comic, poetic or prosaic, and so on.

Yet, in spite of this diversity, all discussions about the novel can, in the last resort, be related to two great themes: commitment versus non-commitment and realism versus idealism. It is on these issues that Communist writers are largely at variance with 'Western' writers and that 'Western' writers have quarrelled among themselves. Sartre campaigned for a number of years in favour of his idea of commitment; Virginia Woolf attacked H. G. Wells and Arnold Bennett because she disagreed with their concept of realism; the contemporary French 'New Novel', with which Robbe-Grillet's name is associated, can be seen as a reaction against commitment and as a search for an original form of realism.

Unfortunately, commitment, non-commitment, realism and idealism are such very ambiguous terms that, at times, they become almost interchangeable.

For Sartre, commitment appears to signify adapting the novel (or any other form of writing) to immediate political ends. The writer should accept responsibility for the society in which he lives, he should evolve a practical philosophy in respect of it, and he should embody that philosophy in his works. If he fails to do all this, he is being cowardly or frivolous. The Communist version of commitment, known as 'Socialist Realism', goes a good deal further and becomes, in fact, a kind of dogmatic idealism. The Communist writer must accept orthodox Neo-Marxist philosophy as true and, while free to point out backslidings, he must give an encouraging overall picture of Communist development, even at the expense of accuracy, because pessimism would conflict with the official basic beliefs.

In a wider sense, commitment is the preliminary acceptance of any philosophy, whether Left Wing or Right Wing, religious or non-religious, and its appropriate form is the moral fable, whether presented as epic, fairy-tale, amorous anecdote, or picaresque adventure. Non-commitment is the refusal to believe that human behaviour is reducible in advance to any definable pattern. These distinctions are clear enough in their simpler formulations, but difficulties arise when we notice that committed writers quite often produce novels that do not correspond to their commitment, or that writers who declare themselves uncommitted are, in fact, accepting some implicit dogma, such as 'art for art's sake'. The paradox of Sartre's position, for instance, is that his committed novels can be read as a demonstration of the failure of commitment. Similarly, most Catholic novelists are working off their heretical tendencies. On the other hand, Huysmans' *Against the Grain*, one of the most disengaged novels ever written, is a kind of propagandist tract for aestheticism.

What it comes to is that a novelist's conscious attitude towards commitment is no sure guide to the artistic quality of his books, to his instinctive feeling for character and plot or to the real message his work contains. After reading a lot about commitment, I would conclude that the only valid policy for the writer is complete commitment to the details of the truth as he sees them at the time of writing, even if they contradict his most cherished convictions. Let him be absolutely sincere in his details and the overall message will take care of itself.

This brings us naturally to realism, one definition of which might be 'the sincere description of the minute particulars of the world'. However, such description is by no means as easy as it first appears. People sometimes imagine that 'reality' is accessible and has only to be transferred faithfully to the novel for 'realism' to be achieved. But a moment's reflection will reveal why the attempt to do this has led to such very different results and to such fierce arguments.

Reality is endlessly complex and, with the best will in the world, no individual, however talented, can see more than a fraction of it. He is limited both by his range of perception as a human being and by his subjective vision as a particular person. Moreover, when the individual is a novelist, he is expressing his vision by means of language, which is an extreme form of shorthand and not at all a one-to-one equivalent for the events of experience. Any writer must trim and arrange his material and concoct a pattern of half-truths by which he hopes to suggest what he considers as major truth. It follows that there can be no such thing as 'objective realism'; there can only be imperfect subjective realism, and this means, in practice, as many forms of realism as there are writers, and the term becomes almost meaningless.

When Virginia Woolf criticised Wells and Bennett for being prosaic, and pleaded for a better rendering of the poetic tremulousness of experience, she was arguing in favour of her brand of realism; she was saying that poetic tremulousness was the quality she herself most wished to bring out. But it so happens that, historically, realism has usually meant insistence on the sordid aspects of life, not on its poetry. This is partly because the term was first used in the nineteenth century with reference to those writers who emphasised the horrors of modern society, and partly because it is often assumed that the sordid is more 'real' than the non-sordid. Actually, since the Middle Ages, the 'idealistic' pastoral or Utopian romance has always been counterbalanced by scurrilous tales and picaresque adventures, which critics have referred to as 'realistic'. However, the latest group of writers to appeal to a concept of realism—the exponents of the French *nouveau roman*—deliberately turn away from many of the features hitherto considered as part of realistic description. They start from the assumption that 'reality' is in the mind and consists as much of imaginings and dreams as of awareness of the external world. Hence a new kind of novel, which offers very little plot or characterisation of the traditional sort, but instead presents a pattern of subjective images, depending on irrational private whim, rather in the manner of abstract painting. By a curious development of the idea of realism, Robbe-Grillet's *In the Labyrinth*, a sophisticated product of the present French school, comes, then, to have the dream-like shadowiness and the thin, formal precision of the old allegorical romance which preceded the rise of the modern novel.

Robbe-Grillet's realism is as different from that of, say, C. P. Snow (or of any of the many novelists of all countries who continue in the more traditional vein) as the diabolical idealism of the Marquis de Sade's violently pornographic moral fable, *One Hundred and Twenty Days in Sodom*, is different from the idealism of that other moral fable, *Little Lord Fauntleroy*. An art form which embraces such extremes can certainly be said to show contrasts of approach.

MICHAEL JOSEPH LTD

privileged to publish for

Doris Lessing

George Lamming

James Baldwin

Keith Waterhouse

Isak Dinesen

Romain Gary

Joyce Cary

two kinds of novel

by MALCOLM BRADBURY

Malcolm Bradbury is a member of the Department of English of the University of Birmingham. His first novel, 'Eating People Is Wrong', was published in 1959.

Despite the fact that a very large number of novels is published in England each year, and that many of our liveliest younger minds seem to turn perfectly naturally to the novel form, the post-war English novel has not been particularly distinguished either in its power to experiment or for its success in defining new human responses to a rapidly changing world. The two things go together, of course; and it is hard not to suspect that this general flatness of the novel has something to do with a thinness and shrillness that one discerns in the English intellectual scene, has to do with a general devaluation of the mind that seems to have occurred in England over this period—a devaluation whose terms might be hinted at when one observes that protest-marching is now assumed to be an *intellectual* mode of expression. There has been, one is inclined to feel, a curious thinning down of conflicts at the level of intellectual debate, an increasing intransigence at a lower, indeed a political, level, and a general refusal to try to test the largest issues of experience and understanding against the conditions of our modern world. The tendency of the modern English novel to rehearse, repetitively and insistently, a number of routines about our alienation and our protest, our fondness for sexuality and our morbid taste for worldly goods, is perhaps evidence of our failure to widen our epistemology through a large act of the literary imagination. It is indeed my own suspicion that we are beginning to doubt the usefulness of the literary imagination, and that it is giving way to another kind of imagination, the sociological imagination, whose epistemology is of a broader yet a very much more descriptive and passive kind.

Thus many of our brighter minds *do* turn to the novel, but curiously often they disappoint us; and in part the reason is that the novel is not, for them, the final or the only form for saying what they want to say—the article and the book review and the poem (and even, as I say, the protest-march) will serve their turn equally well. We do indeed tend to see novel-writing as journeyman work, and postulate for the novel a limited use—a use much more limited than that assumed by the great experimentalists of the period around the turn of the century. The conspicuous tone of the post-war English novel has been that of a flat sociological realism; the only communal response that the novelist seems capable of drawing upon is a kind of generalised cynicism or dissent, and the repeated pattern of the plot seems to be one in which an existentially defined hero, self-contained and a-social, is presented against a society which becomes the butt of his scepticism. In one way, it seems to me, we want to write social novels about anti-social people —and indeed I suspect that part of the novelist's present dilemma is that the predominant novel-form in England, which is broadly social and moral and draws upon a high degree of social consensus, does not easily adapt to an age in which that social and moral consensus is hard to come by. I further suspect that the problem of resolving the issue left open by the liberal optimism of the nineteenth century—the issue of creating an adequate relation between a man and his society when the bonds of goodwill and consensus are loosened—is proving too great; perhaps in the end we are held up by our failure to have any useful concept of the kind of man who can cope with the modern world. Miss Iris Murdoch, in an excellent article 'Against Dryness', recently published in *Encounter*, has suggested as much.

There are, of course, a number of English novelists who have tried for a larger world-view and have taken an experimental approach to the form. Most of these, however, are related to an ideal of the novel and of the writer's rôle which many younger novelists have chosen to repudiate . . . the ideal of the artist as the cosmopolite, as international man, following art as a dedication and taking the form as far as it would go. The international novel which developed in the west during the great age of literary expatriation and literary exile emerged from a faith in the disinterested and dedicated artist, whose province was extra-national and ranged from America in the west to Russia in the east, and whose purposes were to depict whole societies and broad and universal disquiets and anguishes. Such post-war novelists as Samuel Beckett, Lawrence Durrell, and Malcolm Lowry are heirs to this tradition, but it is noticeable that all have direct links with the experimental novelists of the 'twenties, and their modes of life, their assumed audience, and their romantic self-definition are clearly inherited from their mentors, Joyce, Proust, Thomas Wolfe, Scott Fitzgerald. All three published novels before the war, though their reputations have been made after it; they formed their literary careers and their literary values in that atmosphere. All have been expatriates, all are highly conscious artists trying to make explicit highly romantic ideas of art, all manifest the cosmopolitanism, philosophical and moral, of the international writer who has found by travel a view of life he could not have had at home.

By and large, however, the younger English novelists have tended to repudiate this idea of the writer and this mode of art. They have tended to prefer novels without artistic pretensions or elaborate moral apparatus, novels which stake a great deal on social description and the accurate definition of persons often from social classes not fully colonised by the novel as yet. They have tended to make a virtue of provinciality, cultural ignorance, and of their own general scepticism about the world they describe. None of them have experienced the international republic of letters as a fact—except perhaps Iris Murdoch, who deals with intellectuals and cosmopolitan people, manifests an evident debt to the French surrealists, and has a professional variety about her work, and Angus Wilson—and most show little desire to renew, at anything higher than the P.E.N. club level, the contacts severed by the war. France has ceased to be the country of Flaubert and Proust and has become the place where one went bicycling and had one's saddlebag pinched. Italy is no longer the centre of an ideal of art but a country of motor-scooters and bottom-nipping men. And the sense that the artists of the west were linked together by a common literary endeavour has faded as rapidly as has the notion that the literary imagination is a self-governing mode of discovery. Though the French novel has gone through an experimental phase, there has been little response in England in the way of influence; as C. P. Snow and William Cooper have remarked, with some pleasure and pride, the English novel seems nowadays to have thrown out that sort of thing.

One of the consequences of this situation is that many of the best and most original novels now being written in English are being produced in the United States, where the notion of art as an autonomous way of knowing still has considerable strength. If on the one hand this tends to make artists self-engrossed, self-conscious and neurotic, on the other hand a general excitement does still attach to literary exploration. Salinger's anguished attempts to reconcile love and squalor in fragile intellectual heroes, and Bellow's endeavour to find in man some essential spring of nobility, are of a largeness which few English writers care to match. Perhaps this largeness has to do with power and precedence —has to do, in fact, with the freshness of experience that is felt in countries pushing hardest into the future. The great period of literary expatriation in the late nineteenth century was based on a fairly realistic sense of international cultural relations—it was founded on a conviction that art could only be written in places which ministered to it and that these places bore some relation to the centres of economic and political as well as cultural power. But of course cultural heritage does have an independent existence; the American novel is founded on a tradition of cultural borrowing which

James thought the characteristic quality of the American literary mind. It is this perhaps that accounts for its receptivity, and for its present activity. The stream of the international European novel has fed into American literature; one feels, in reading Bellow, that here is a novelist who has drawn in equal parts on Dostoyevsky and Dreiser, and the intonations of Kafka and Camus recur frequently in the younger American novelists.

To some extent, I think, the English novel just now falls short of all this, both in its achievement and in its current general atmosphere. And yet, I think, the situation has been sensed, and the lost links with Europe may be part of a general change of cultural alliances which points toward a new kinship with America. The circulation of American literature in England, the growing contacts as English writers go to America and American ones come here, and the common confessions among the younger English novelists of debt to American writers like Hemingway, Fitzgerald, and Salinger, suggest that a new international literary unit is being formed, and that it is not one in which the English writer feels the superior party. All this is not surprising; Americanisation tends to take place in cultural fields as it does in economic ones, and as the problems of highly industrialised capitalist democracy, and the transition from puritan individualism to a mass-society, are confronted here, so one tends to turn to American cultural solutions. It is this that in part explains the phenomenon of the English beat poet, the cult of the writer in jeans and in protest. And other factors reinforce the situation, particularly the fact of the Anglo-American publishing connection, which means that the writer nowadays has a sense of an Anglo-American audience. The international novel about the Englishman in America is clearly a response to the new audience and the increased facilities for the experience; and I, struggling with just such a novel, cannot but feel conscious that the theme tends to involve the desire to escape from the social novel as a form. The characteristic English novel is, I think, social, and assumes a relatively stable social order, a fairly high degree of social consensus both between the characters within the book and between author and reader outside it, and a more or less closed world. Religious, social, political, and intellectual standards are not matters of elaborate debate; they can be taken for granted. And these public values broadly support existing society. But a paring away of this consensus has taken place in the world at large, and even in England—a society, one might venture to suggest, whose chief value lies in its power to create and evoke consensus—we tend more and more in our description of men to point toward an existential centre. Tocqueville saw this as the characteristic democratic subject for literature; it would be about 'man alone'. And indeed fiction in this mode has long been written in America—the populist novel, concerned less with communities than individual states of mind, seeking more to confront man with the large forces of nature than with his duties as a social animal, tending toward romance and symbolism rather than toward realism and social delineation, has been a characteristic American form, the form of *Moby Dick* and *Huckleberry Finn*. A parallel tradition does exist in England—in the Brontës, Hardy, and Lawrence (writers who all seem to be undergoing a revival)—and it may be that as society grows more complex and sociology more common the English novel will be pushed further in this direction. But other methods of development and presentation do seem likely to emerge if it is thought important that they should. As it is, the epistemological problem I am describing seems a characteristic one in an intellectual scene where too many minds are trapped by the limits of the political imagination; the literary imagination has always promised larger things.

I am all too conscious that these jottings do not represent adequately the pleasure I take from many young English writers or the kind of promise I find there. Yet I must confess that, broadly speaking, I feel that we shall go on looking for some time yet to the European novel and the American novel, which is curiously kin to it, for the richest literary nourishment.

day two : scottish writing today

The Second Day of the Conference is devoted to a discussion of contemporary Scottish writing. To introduce, and to provide a background for, this discussion, David Daiches here defines historically the Scots literary tradition, David Craig surveys the achievement of Scottish writing in this century, Walter Keir writes on Hugh MacDiarmid, still the dominant figure on the contemporary Scottish literary scene, and Edwin Morgan discusses the problems and difficulties confronting the young Scots writer today.

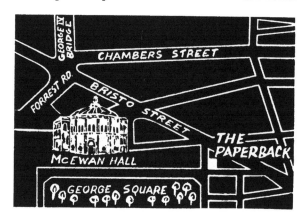

the scottish literary tradition

by DAVID DAICHES

Dr. Daiches has lectured at several British and American universities. He is now Dean of the School of English and American Studies at the University of Sussex. Among his many publications are 'The Novel and the Modern World' (1939), 'Robert Burns' (1950), and 'A Critical History of English Literature' (1960).

Is Scottish literature part of English literature, or is there a separate identifiable Scottish literary tradition with respect to which Scottish writers see themselves and place themselves? There is no simple answer to what may seem like a simple question. A small nation living on the doorstep of a larger and more powerful one, and speaking a kindred language, is bound to be strongly influenced by the literary modes and practices of its potent neighbour. But this is only one factor in the situation. In 1603 Scotland's king inherited the throne of England and came south to rule both kingdoms, depriving his Scottish kingdom at a blow both of the royal patronage of the arts and of the presence of some of its most accomplished practising poets, who followed their king to London. Already the Reformation in Scotland had turned the eyes of many Scotsmen to a reformed England and away from Catholic France, Scot-

land's traditional ally, and this association had a rapid effect on the literary language. From 1707, when the two kingdoms were fused into one by the Union of Parliaments and an independent Scottish Parliament—indeed, independent Scottish political life—ceased to exist, Anglicising pressure became steadily greater and Scotsmen tended more and more to write in English largely for an English audience.

Language was not of course the only problem, but it was a basic and, in a sense, a symbolic one. In the Middle Ages the literary language of those Scotsmen who did not live in predominantly Gaelic-speaking areas was what we call Scots and they called 'Inglis'. This language began by being identical with that spoken and written in northern England as far south as the Humber—it was, that is, a northern form of English. As Scotland found itself as a nation and the *mélange* of Scots, Picts, Strathclyde Britons, Norsemen, and Anglo-Saxons gradually formed into a people with two major languages—Scots and Gaelic—a distinctive Scottish literary tradition developed. By the fifteenth century the language of the non-Gaelic areas had entered the phase we call Middle Scots, and this was worked up by the Scottish writers of the period into a highly complex and extremely versatile literary language. This was the language of Scotland's great poets of her Golden Age—of Robert Henryson, whose *Fables* show a delicately ironic use of realistic detail and whose *Testament of Cresseid* is a moving and beautifully modulated sequel to Chaucer's *Troilus and Cresseid*; of William Dunbar, the great idiosyncratic poet of medieval Edinburgh with his technical virtuosity, his startling range of mood and of vocabulary, his vivid sense of the moment and his haunting sense of eternity; of Gavin Douglas, whose translation of the *Aeneid* is a great European achievement. The language of these poets was by now distinctively Scottish. Though they had learned from Chaucer, they were often quite un-Chaucerian in outlook and technique. They belonged to Europe as well as to Scotland, and produced their own Scottish versions of European themes.

The Golden Age lasted roughly from 1430 until 1513, when the disastrous Battle of Flodden undid much of the unifying and ordering work of the first four Stuart kings. In this period Scottish literature, using Middle Scots as its language, exhibited a self-confidence, a poise, a maturity, and a national character that have never since been equalled. Religious and political conflicts of the middle and late sixteenth century then darken the picture, but even so we can trace in this period new developments in the tradition of court literature and the strengthening of a new popular literature which was to constitute the major literary resource with the disappearance of a Scottish Court in 1603. After 1707, with Scotland officially a part of 'Great Britain' and Scottish writers (such as the poet James Thomson) migrating to England to seek their fortunes there or writing in English for a 'British' audience, the prospects for a distinctive Scottish literature seemed meagre. Scotsmen learned standard English at school, and wrote it if not altogether as a foreign language at least with a certain formality and, as it were, at a distance. They still for the most part *spoke* Scots, that northern form of English which, while losing steadily many of its distinguishing elements in vocabulary, retained its distinctive pronunciation, idiom, and usage. A truly vital literary language must have its roots deep in the living spoken language of the people, however much it may add or refine or enrich. A people that tended to speak and feel in one language and to write in another—even though the two languages were closely related historically—were deprived of the opportunity of producing a literature in which the *whole man*, the total complex of thinking and feeling personality, could find expression. As a result there developed a humorous or regional or patronising or in some other way limited use of dialect Scots, with English reserved for more formal and more serious writing.

The collapse of Scots into a series of regional dialects was the inevitable result of the decline of a full-blooded Scots literature. Scottish patriots turned with antiquarian zeal to reprinting and editing specimens of older Scottish poetry written when Scots was a true literary language; they turned also to collecting and circulating Scottish songs and popular poetry in an endeavour to keep alive some sense of a living popular native literature. Allan Ramsay engaged in both these activities, and he also wrote vividly realistic poems in Scots dealing with low life, with Edinburgh sights and sounds, or with rustic festivities. But Ramsay was a symptom of the confusion of early eighteenth-century Scottish culture. He was at the same time an ardent Jacobite and a prudent citizen; an admirer and imitator of Addison and Steele, and a propagandist for the characteristically Scottish in literature; a zealous editor on patriotic grounds of the great poetry of the Scottish Middle Ages, and a vulgar mutilator and desecrator of that literature; a worker for a Scottish literary Renaissance, and a tasteless vulgarian who would ornament and 'improve' old popular Scottish poems into monstrosities; a lively and appealing poet in a popular Scots idiom, and a seeker after the elegance and gentility of the English Augustan Age.

But the eighteenth century has also been called a Golden Age of Scottish literature, and with some reason. The language problem did not bother philosophers and historians, who could profit by the discipline of having to put their thoughts into a formal language which was not directly related to the language of their childhood speech. 'This is the historical age, and we are the historical people,' David Hume exclaimed proudly, and with some justification. The achievement of Francis Hutcheson, Adam Smith, David Hume, and many other Scottish philosophers, historians, and literary critics made eighteenth-century Scotland known throughout Europe as a centre of literature and learning. This was a genuinely Scottish achievement, and it is not too much of a distortion to see the English writings of these men as comparable to the Latin prose writings of medieval writers on these topics. They despised their own vernacular, as many medieval writers had done. Thus, while some writers and scholars were collecting and imitating older Scottish poetry, both 'art' poetry and folk poetry, in a mood of patriotic rediscovery, others were seeking to establish their greatness as Scotsmen by producing their thoughts to the world in standard English and actually published lists of 'Scotticisms' so that aspiring writers should know what to avoid.

The creative side of Ramsay's work was developed in a more original and more artistically responsible way by Robert Fergusson, who drew on his Aberdeenshire origins, his Fifeshire student days, and his Edinburgh domicile to construct a Scots that was more than a single regional dialect. In his tragically brief career (he died in the public Bedlam of Edinburgh in 1774 at the age of 24) Fergusson produced some brilliant Scots poems descriptive and evocative of Edinburgh life. The world he moved in was not Hume's, and inevitably his kind of contribution had 'low' associations. The split in Scottish culture becomes very clear when we set the Edinburgh 'literati', as they called themselves (the philosophers and critics who wrote in standard English and worked hard to eliminate 'Scotticisms' from their writing), beside this gay, doomed young man who single-handed almost created a new urban tradition in Scottish poetry.

Fergusson's successor was Robert Burns, but Burns had different origins. A countryman, brought up in a rural community, he was in touch from the beginning with the old Scottish folk tradition. His formal education was in English literature, but he was in intimate contact with the tensions and shifting attitudes of a rural society in a time of rapid change. If his very earliest poetry was love poetry in the tradition of Scottish folk song, he first showed his real strength as a poet in satirical poems dealing with local affairs and local personalities. He learned much from the eighteenth-century English poets. But he learned more from traditions of Scottish poetry, both folk and 'art', that he acquired as he grew up, and he was inspired by Fergusson's Scots poems to emulation. In his brilliant satires and verse epistles he showed his real strength—his power to create a Scots poetry that dealt vividly and centrally with genuine Scottish themes. Later, when he embarked on the task of renovating and re-creating Scottish folk song, he produced a body of songs, each set to a known air, that showed his uncanny gift for realising the given moment of experience in precise and passionate utterance. His language was partly the Scots of his native Ayrshire, partly a Scots he learned from Fergusson and from Ramsay's and other editors' collections of older poets; sometimes it was English tipped with Scots; sometimes (rarely successfully) it was wholly eighteenth-century English. He deliberately took advantage of the sentimental interest in primitive and supposedly primitive poetry then prevailing among Edinburgh critics to present himself as a 'Heaven-taught ploughman', a simple unlettered peasant, which was far from the truth—he was an educated man and a sophisticated artist. The critics encouraged him to write a declamatory sentimental poetry which they considered appropriate to a peasant poet and which they highly esteemed, but though he could not avoid giving in to these pressures in some degree, he resisted them for the most part, and his satires, his verse letters, and his best songs are evidence of that resistance and the real proofs of his genius.

It was an Indian Summer of the Scottish literary tradition that Burns created, for there was less and less in the life of the community that was able to nourish a Scots poetry in which the whole man spoke. Even Burns was restricted in some important respects by the confusions in the society and culture in which he worked. His successors, looking back nostalgically from an increasingly industrialised Scotland on his poetry of rural life, concentrated on and exaggerated his sentimental side, with the result that, through no fault of his own, his influence in the nineteenth century was almost wholly pernicious. Corroding nostalgia became increasingly the vice of Scottish literature, both prose and poetry, and one of the aims of the Scottish Renaissance of the present century has been to create a more astringent literature that really confronts experience as it is found to be in modern Scotland. To do this, poets had to get behind the precarious balance represented by Burns's achievement to the poets of the Golden Age of the fifteenth century, when Scots was a full-blooded literary language and Scottish literature was both fully national and fully European. The cry 'Back to Dunbar' was thus no mere antiquarian slogan, but the proclamation of a genuine literary ideal. To re-create a Scots language by deliberately synthesising elements from modern regional dialects and from older Scottish literature, including the Middle Scots poets, is obviously not a solution open to every modern Scottish writer; for all the special ways of handling English which come naturally to a Scot brought up and educated in Scotland, it can hardly be said today that standard English is not the native language of most Scotsmen. Yet English modes will not always express the Scottish experience. The founder of the modern Scottish Renaissance, Hugh MacDiarmid, whose position as one of the great Scottish poets is now universally recognised, wrote some of his most impressive poetry in a synthetic Scots, but his later work, though ever more fiercely Scottish in feeling, is written in English. A few poets still write in synthetic Scots, sometimes impressively, but whether such a language can solve the problems of the Scottish literary sensibility in the modern world on any large scale is a matter for debate.

These notes have ignored the Scottish novel, which developed after the fragmentation of Scottish culture was well under way, but it is worth observing that Walter Scott was not merely a romantic escapist who invented the historical novel; his best novels, those dealing with seventeenth- and eighteenth-century Scottish history, explored the relations between tradition and progress in Scotland and the inevitable shifting of the possibilities of heroism from the active to the prudential sphere. They thus touch on a paradox which is central to Scotland's dilemma. Nothing has been said either of the Scottish Gaelic tradition, whose story is rather different. The older Gaelic poetry of the formal bardic schools—which was part of the culture of Gaeldom as a whole and was not merely Scottish—gave way in the seventeenth century to a Scottish Gaelic poetry independent of the formal rhetorical training of the Irish schools, and in the eighteenth century produced (largely but not altogether under the stimulus of Jacobite feeling) a minor Scottish Gaelic literary Renaissance, of which the most distinguished figure was Alexander Macdonald. The revival of an original Scottish Gaelic poetry in our own time by such impressive poets as Somhairle Maclean and George Campbell Hay is testimony to the tenacity of the Gaelic tradition in Scotland, though the future of the language remains problematical. No single solution to the very real problems facing the Scottish writer has been found, and it is not likely that one will be found. But the last thirty years or so have seen some immensely exciting developments. The sentimentalism and complacency of the post-Burnsians have been successfully challenged, one really great poet has emerged, and the problems are out in the open.

scottish literature this century

by DAVID M CRAIG

Dr. Craig is Organising Tutor for the Workers' Educational Association, Yorkshire North District. He is the author of 'Scottish Literature and the Scottish People, 1680-1830', published in 1961.

Scottish literature this century has seen one whole age give place to another. George Douglas Brown's *The House with the Green Shutters* was published in 1901. Yet it seems as remote to us now as *Wuthering Heights*. It was a sort of imperfect classic, not quite emerged from a raw state, about the strains put on feelings and relationships by the effort to succeed in a harshly competitive community. Like many a classic from the mid-nineteenth to the early twentieth century —*Dombey and Son*, Giovanni Verga's *Mastro-Don Guesaldo*, Thomas Mann's *Buddenbrooks*, Gorky's *The Artamonovs* a little later—Brown's novel shows the energy and lust for social power that flowed into business in an age of breakneck capitalist growth, though he in rural Ayrshire saw only the fringe of the process and was too at war with himself to focus such matters clearly.

Thirty years later, there came out of the Mearns (Kincardineshire) a man with as passionate an anger as Brown at the life his people lived—Lewis Grassic Gibbon. As a conscious follower of Brown, he was determined to re-create Scotland's image of itself by replacing the falsely simple imitations of the pokier sides of village life, at once patronising and sentimental, that Scottish writers (especially ministers) had specialised in since the death of Scott (1832). The classic of the kind was Barrie. Gibbon aimed at something between the over-mellow and Brown's savage gloom, and he achieved it in his trilogy: *Sunset Song* (1932), set in the farms, *Cloud Howe* (1933), in a small burgh, and *Grey Granite* (1934), in the city.

Gibbon was so at one with the people that he could give in an effortless flow the wholesome sociality of their life as well as its coarse rigours. He shows us the intellect of the people—two key characters are a socialist small-holder and a free-thinking miller; and he shows us how mercilessly history moulded their lives. We can never forget the image of the young farmer back on leave from the Great War, 'the coarse hair that sprang like short bristles all over his head, the neck with its red and angry circle above the collar of the khaki jacket, a great half-healed scar across the back of his hand glinted putrescent blue'.

Gibbon himself had emigrated to London, and a terrible nostalgia tended to swamp his writing and expose the reader to the most helpless pathos. But at its best his style moves with the very energies of popular speech, comedy, and song. Here is the death of an old landlady from *Grey Granite*:

And suddenly Ma's lips ceased to twist and slobber with their blowings of brownish spume, her hand in Chris's slackened with a little jerk and she stepped from the bed and out of the house and up long stairs that went wandering to Heaven like the stairs on Windmill Brae. And she met at the Gates St Peter himself, in a lum hat and leggings, looking awful stern, the father of all the Wee Free ministers, and he held up his hand and snuffled through his nose and asked in GAWD's name was she one of the Blessed? And Ma Cleghorn said she was blest if she knew—*Let's have a look at this Heaven of yours*. And she pushed him aside and took a keek in, and there was God with a plague in one hand and a war and a thunderbolt in the other and the Christ in glory with the angels bowing, and a scraping and banging of harps and drums, ministers thick as a swarm of bluebottles, no sight of Jim and no sight of

Jesus, only the Christ, and she wasn't impressed. And she said to St Peter *This is no place for me*, and turned and went striding into the mists and across the fire-tipped clouds to her home.

This is a sheer folk-story, the old devastating irreverence of Burns linked now to a passionate rationalism that impels a satire more fearless than Britain had known since the seventeenth century.

To write well about the Highlands must be hard. The terrible devastations of its society both impoverish the subject-matter and unleash emotions that can barely be coped with. Fionn MacColla's novel *And The Cock Crew* (1945), about the Clearances (those ruthless evictions of crofters in the later eighteenth and early nineteenth centuries), is clearly a sincere book. But I cannot pretend that it leaves a concerted impression at all proportionate to the evident effort to rouse our sympathies. Like his recent fragment on the War of Independence, *Scottish Noel* (1957), it is too descriptive—a spate of imagery that seems to compensate for a lack of inward insight into its subject.

Neil Gunn, a contemporary of Gibbon, wrote stark novels of Highland fisher-folk and crofters that were probably influenced by J. M. Synge (the tragic Synge). But Gunn must always be inflating his material, stylising or orating where simple freshness is wanted : the farm woman in *Morning Tide* (1932) is never 'Mother' or 'Mrs. Mackay' but 'the mother'—archetypal, and featureless. *The Drinking Well* (1946) has passages that strive to symbolise how it is that so much Scottish talent has felt starved and isolated or gone to seed. But constantly it collapses into the usual ready-made nationalist Problems, or else escapes into mysticism.

Again and again—in J. D. Scott's *The End of an Old Song*, in Robin Jenkins' *The Thistle and the Grail* (both 1954)—we come to a point where the writer puts us off, as a substitute for real analysis, with one or other of the well-tried Scottish diagnoses—Calvinism, the provincial, the split in our language. It is as though they were determined to remain national or 'different' even if they no longer really feel it. Perhaps it would have taken a Henry James to pick his way surefootedly through this quaking ground of national consciousness and over-consciousness, or a D. H. Lawrence to give our life straight and strong, undistorted by preconceived ideas.

However, modern Scottish literature asks more than do English, American, or French to be judged by its poetry rather than its fiction. Sixty years ago we had little but echoes of Tennyson and imitations of R. L. Stevenson's imitations of Burns. But by 1925 Hugh MacDiarmid had emerged as a master poet, able (like Yeats in Ireland) to turn his every experience into poetry that moved beautifully from point to point, established its own distinctive rhythms, and struck out images that remain forever in the mind as symbols of some of the characteristically modern themes. He had no forerunner, unlike Gibbon, and had to take his language from speech and from medieval poets and a nineteenth century dictionary of Scots. His genius with words not only created thirty or forty masterly short poems and one amazing long sequence but, geared to the driving-power of his fervent nationalism, imposed the writing of poetry in synthetic Scots as *the* serious literary mode in Scotland for the succeeding quarter-century.

MacDiarmid is presented at proper length elsewhere in this programme. But to survey this half-century in our literature without stressing his crucial and dominating rôle would be inexcusably misleading—much more so than to pass over Lawrence's rôle in English fiction or even T. S. Eliot's in English poetry. Let me at least quote, from his *Second Hymn to Lenin* (1935), a poem so fine that it is rarely out of my mind for many days at a time—'Lo! A Child is Born':

. . . Then I thought of the whole world. Who cares for its travail
And seeks to encompass it in like loving-kindness and peace ?
There is a monstrous din of the sterile who contribute nothing
To the great end in view, and the future fumbles,
A bad birth, not like the child in that gracious home
Heard in the quietness turning in its mother's womb,
A strategic mind already, seeking the best way
To present himself to life, and at last, resolved,

Springing into history quivering like a fish,
Dropping into the world like a ripe fruit in due time.—
But where is the Past to which Time, smiling through her tears
At her new-born son, can turn crying: 'I love you'?

By itself this passage shows two essentials of our poetry: it has had to keep itself in being by most deliberate efforts of will (suggested here by 'strategic mind'), and it has been as much at home in English as in Scots. For that is in fact the nature of our speech and language—sometimes dialect, sometimes educated and therefore, inevitably, English.

That poem is also progressive. MacDiarmid, as a Marxist, is looking out over the whole of man's massive struggle to develop. Few of our other poets have had full enough minds to supply grist for this mill of language that has ground so fine. But it is striking to see, as one reads through Maurice Lindsay's anthology of *Modern Scottish Poetry* (1946), how time after time the outstanding lyrics are progressive—against inequality and exploitation, against war.

Sorley Maclean writes in Gaelic (translated by Douglas Young):

> My een are nae on Calvary
> or the Bethlehem they praise,
> but on shitten *back-lands* in Glesga toun   *tenements*
> where growan life decays. . . .

Adam Drinan (Joseph Macleod) writes a poem called 'Successful Scot' that is in direct line with Burns though it is in English:

> By adding figure to figure
>   you have developed never,
> you have just grown bigger and bigger
>   like this wee wort from the heather
>   and size is all you have got.
>
> Your mind set towards London,
>   your belly pushing to success. . . .

George Campbell Hay's magnificent 'Thonder They Ligg' (also trans. from Gaelic by Young) commemorates the appalling numbers of our islanders who lost their lives in the Merchant and Royal Navies fighting England's wars:

> 'Wheesht, woman, wheesht, and *deavena* me.   *don't bother*
> My wae's the mair to see ye *greet*.   *weep*
> The ship brak down under our feet,
> life gaed aff, and memorie wi 't.
> London slew me, weary faa 't,
> *connacht* the een that never saw it. . . .'   *ruined*

This fine progressive tradition is partly a product of the militant Thirties, like Auden and MacNeice in England, Brecht in Germany. But partly it emerged because Scotland, a small nation with a bent for independence, has for long been a cradle of radicalism. Red Clydeside was a well-head of the most advanced socialism in the age that formed MacDiarmid—the Great War and its aftermath.

In general, it seems to me, the specialist-nationalist concentration on revived language as indispensable for a national literature has done little more than conceal shallow inspiration under a crust of seemingly flavoursome and characterful diction. Synthetic language does excel in translation, where what is needed is not so much a natural style as a special new equivalent for the foreign thing. So Douglas Young used medieval Scots to make up an extraordinarily felicitous equivalent for the French of Valéry's *Cimetière Marin* (in his *A Braird o Thristles*, 1947), for example—

> But in their nicht, wechtit wi marble stane,
> a *drowie* fowk doun at the tree-ruits lain   *indistinct*
> hae sideit wi you in slaw solemnitie.
>
> They hae *dwyneit* intil a thick nonentitie,   *diminished*
> the reid clay drank the whyte identitie. . . .

That is the more elaborate or Metaphysical kind of language. Frequently, Scots survives in our poetry as the kind of 'unanswerable' simplicity that comes time and again from folk poets but is seemingly impossible now in English and was possible for Yeats only after 40 years of struggle. This simple language can be richly bawdy, notably in section XIII of Sydney Goodsir Smith's *Under the Eildon Tree* (1948), an attempt at a Scots *Waste Land* but successful only, I think, in the bawdy vein:

> —Ah, she was a bonnie cou!
> Saxteen, maybe sevinteen, nae mair,
> Her mither in attendance, comme il faut

Pour les jeunes filles bien élevées,
   Drinkan like a bluidie whaul tae! . . .
   Her een were, naiturallie, expressionless,
Blank as *chuckie-stanes*, like the bits   *pebbles*
O' blae-green gless ye find by the sea. . . .

Or the simplicity can be perfectly straight, perfectly earnest
and sincere as few modern Western styles are capable of,
for example the last poem from John Manson's fine sequence
'Poems of an Undefined Love' (*We Must Alter All the
Words*, 1954):

   I'm no playan the game o love.
   Ye may say
   We were no engaged
   And only going out
   Afore the public
   But in the hert
   Neither were we disengaged
   And ye lit him pit his mooth there.

And in the best new poems I have seen recently, Alan
Jackson's *Underwater Wedding* (1961), a recognisably Scottish English—terse, full of straightfaced sarcasm—is used
to suggest the experience of being fed-up with worn-out
family relationships.

   Thus the writers native to this part of the world
continue to create things characteristic of their own community; although, inevitably, our basis, our body of distinctive experiences, grows narrower and narrower as we become
absorbed into the centralised British culture.

*Note.—I shall be criticised for omitting drama. But unless you live in
Glasgow or Edinburgh, it is impossible to see such good new Scottish
plays as there are. At my one seeing of it, Roddy Macmillan's play in
Glaswegian, 'All in Good Faith' (1954), was clearly a genuine and
vital piece; and I should think that a reading of it (only a fragment
has been printed, in the 'Saltire Review', 2) would confirm its place
in the strongest line of Western drama—the line that includes Arthur
Miller, Arnold Wesker, and Shelagh Delaney.*

hugh macdiarmid

by W A S KEIR

Walter Keir lectures on English literature at the University of Aberdeen.

'Hugh MacDiarmid', well named Scotland's 'Scarlet Eminence', began writing over forty years ago, and he has dominated the Scottish literary scene ever since. This does not mean, however, that he is in any sense a member of the literary establishment, or that he conforms to any conventional conception of a grand old man of letters. Very much the reverse is true. All his life he has been a stormy petrel, an outsider, a fighter, and a rebel, taking as his motto from the very beginning Thomas Hardy's declaration that 'literature is the written expression of revolt against accepted things', while politically and socially he wants nothing more, and nothing less, than completely 'to reverse the existing order'. To further this aim he has espoused causes as various as Social Credit, Scottish Nationalism—he was one of the founders of the Scottish Nationalist Party—and Communism. He has been a tireless advocate of internationalism while also declaring in one of his most famous utterances:

> The rose of all the world is not for me.
> I choose for my part
> Only the little white rose of Scotland,
> Which smells sharp and sweet, and breaks the heart.

His cast of mind has been shaped by people as different as John Davidson, Charles Doughty, Rainer Maria Rilke—and Lenin. He ceaselessly campaigned for a return to Scots as a poetic medium in the twenties, abandoned it in the thirties when, inevitably, it proved inadequate for what he wanted to say, and then, leaving behind him his bewildered disciples, turned to a poetry of science and fact, to what he calls 'world-view poetry', and to experiments in the direction of a new world language. At the same time he has persistently argued for a return to, and extension of, Gaelic. And his loves have been as violent as his hates, chief amongst which is England: '*Who's Who* has long given my hobby as "Anglophobia"', he writes in his autobiography, *Lucky Poet*. 'But it is a great deal more than a mere hobby. It is my very life.' In other words he appears to many people a mass of contradictions, but in fact he is one of the very few to whom one can legitimately apply that overworked saying of Whitman's—'You say I contradict myself? Very well, then, I contradict myself. I am large, I contain multitudes' —this is his case taking the form of

> I'll hae nae hauf-way hoose, but aye be whaur
> Extremes meet—it's the only way I ken
> To dodge the curst conceit o' bein' richt
> That damns the vast majority o' men.

But MacDiarmid's eclecticism, his celebration of 'the boustrophedon of heaven and hell' is far less the confused thinking and abrogation of logic it is often represented than an attitude comparable to Blake's 'Without contraries is no progression', Rilke's 'Wir sind nicht einig', or—MacDiarmid's lavish use of esoteric quotation must be infectious—the Sinic sages alternations of Yin and Yang. In which connection, and just in passing, I might also point out that when he uses the word 'lucky' in the title of his autobiography, 'it embraces both good luck and bad'.

But now for a few facts, though it is not my intention to give here anything approaching a life. He was born at Langholm, Dumfriesshire, in 1892, and given the name of Christopher Murray Grieve, he went to the local school, and he spent his youth there. Now three things about this early period are particularly significant, and left their mark on much that was to come. Firstly, this area of Scotland has for long had a reputation, sometimes too self-consciously exploited, of individuality and independence. Secondly, he came of working-class stock. And thirdly, he was born in a library, or as near to it as makes no difference. 'My father', he writes, 'was a rural postman . . . and we lived in the post office buildings. The library, the nucleus of which had been left by Thomas Telford, the famous engineer, was upstairs. I had constant access to it.' And it was this library of about twelve thousand volumes, though it was poor in Scottish literature, which was 'the great determining factor' in his youth, which first stimulated his 'immoderate and hydroptique thirst for learning', and which conditioned him to accept as his own Rilke's dictum, 'the poet must know everything'. His own poetry, however, began more modestly when he was on service during the first world war at Salonika and elsewhere. And the end of that war saw him back in Scotland, and for a time at Edinburgh University. Much more important than this, however, on his own confession he came back to Scotland knowing little about it and even less of its literature, but determined to find out. He has had many different kinds of jobs since then, teaching, journalism, manual work—he was in the Clyde shipyards during the second world war—he has been literary editor of Orage's *New Age* in London and he has isolated himself at Whalsay in Orkney, he has travelled widely, particularly in what are now known as the Iron Curtain countries, and he has met or corresponded with most of the great literary figures of his time, but throughout everything this has been his central quest. 'No matter where it ranges', he writes in *Lucky Poet*, 'all my work comes home to Scotland'. But it 'comes home' in the very reverse of a provincial or narrow way. Founding in 1922 *The Scottish Chapbook*, the first periodical of what was soon to be known as the Scottish Renaissance movement, the motto he chose was 'Not traditions—precedents', and chief among its declared aims was 'to bring Scottish literature into closer touch with current European tendencies'. Throughout his career MacDiarmid has emphasised the importance of this, and has led the way to an appreciation of such writers as Rilke, Stefan George, Valéry, Pasternak, Blok, Mayakovsky, and Lorca, long before they were known to all but a tiny handful of people in this country.

So there are two sides to MacDiarmid's work, and to the Scottish Renaissance. To begin with he used Scots and wrote chiefly lyrics. This is the period of *Sangschaw* (1925), and *Penny Wheep* (1926). But in 1926 he also published *A Drunk Man Looks at The Thistle*, a satirical, mordant, boozy, and very acute analysis of the state of Scotland, followed a year later by a prose work, *Albyn*, both of which clearly show the way the wind is blowing. As he wrote in *Albyn* of the Scottish Renaissance, what 'began as a purely literary movement . . . of necessity speedily acquired political and the religious bearings'. What in fact he really wanted, as Sydney Goodsir Smith has since written, was 'nothing less than a national regeneration in all realms of thought and life'. But the full extent of the revolution MacDiarmid wanted to bring about, and one which goes far beyond the boundaries of Scotland, is his insistence that the most fundamental requirement of all is 'to liberate ourselves from that pseudo-religious mental climate which keeps the harmonies and solutions of our writers on so contemptibly shallower a level than the conflicts and tragedies which encompass our lives'. Seen in the light of this remark, and bearing in mind the shocking economic and cultural conditions prevailing in Scotland, MacDiarmid's conversion to Communism, and his desire for an altogether new kind of poetry to replace lyrical doodling in the margin while the face of the world was being transformed, were, if not inevitable, at least understandable. And for a new dialectic a new form was necessary, and a new approach to language.

The attempt to forge a 'synthetic' Scots, by which was meant not something artificial, but a synthesis or amalgam of Scots, was, however, doomed to fail from the start, partly for the reason John Spiers gives, because neither MacDiarmid himself, nor anyone else, speaks it, and partly because for obvious historical reasons working over a couple of centuries, Scots just didn't have the vocabulary to cope with the modern world. But for the time being MacDiarmid persevered with it, in the first two Hymns to Lenin (1931 and 1932), and in parts of *To Circumjack Cencrastus* (1930), *Scots Unbound and Other Poems* (1932), and *Stony Limits and*

Other Poems (1934), all of which are also exploratory of theme and form. As he writes of the two last, *Scots Unbound* and *Stony Limits*, 'Both were largely experimental, the first in extended use of *synthetic Scots* but also of modern scientific terminology, and the second in an endeavour to employ recondite elements of the English vocabulary. Each in its different but complementary way marked steps in the transition from my earlier volumes of lyrics towards my later "world-view" poems.' Equally important, nearly all the poems of this period are concerned with what in *Lucky Poet* MacDiarmid calls 'the restless spirit of man; the energy of thought which transforms the world'. And most important of all, MacDiarmid is now moving towards a completely new aesthetic, the best description of which is given by Burns Singer in an article in *Encounter*, March 1957. 'MacDiarmid', Singer writes, 'has tried to revive the ancient concept of the poet as the universal sage versed in every subject . . . the accumulation of two millennia of historical speculation and research are enough to knock the bottom out of any such pretension, and to explode any previous notions of heroic form. Therefore, reasons MacDiarmid, a new form must be made and its first requirement is that it should contain all knowledge. Other formal considerations, even such basic ones as unity and intelligibility, become negligible when set alongside this impossible imperative. He has tried to create a heroic form, primitive, didactic, universal. The heroes are not men, as they were in Homer. Only the fact has the heroic prerogative of victory.' Now none of this makes for easy reading. Nor does his emphasis on fact: 'I am always stressing the vital importance of *fact*', MacDiarmid writes in the chapter, 'The Ideas Behind My Work' in *Lucky Poet*,

Of thorough documentation.
I am with the new writers who waste no words
On manifestos but are getting down
To the grim business of documentation.

Grim indeed, some critics will say. And again, in 'The Kind of Poetry I Want', also in *Lucky Poet* but now (1962) published separately, he writes that 'above all what I want is a poetry

'Full of august reverberations of world-literature and world history.'

But where does one stop? And again, in *In Memoriam James Joyce* (1955), he writes of himself as

Collecting up all these essences
Into a complex conception of all things,
An intricately cut gem-stone of myriad facets,
That is yet, miraculously, a whole.

But is it a whole? Too often the 'myriad facets' dazzle—or dull—the sight, quotations multiply, illustrations fertilise, cross-breed, and proliferate, and the essence, the unity, is lost.

In his later poetry, then, but leaving aside that magnificent piece of flyting, *The Battle Continues* (1957), he has tried to do something more ambitious than anyone else this century, something bigger than even Joyce or Pound. But like them, I think, he has been misled by a false aesthetic. The attempt to 'include everything', which was Joyce's also, is surely bound to fail, and one sympathises with that sensitive critic who in the end wondered sadly if, after all, *Ulysses* was 'a monument of artifice rather than of art'. And one sympathises, too, with Robert Graves, who, apropos Pound's Chinese Ideograms, commented that as far as he was concerned they might as well have been borrowed from the nearest tea-chest. But much more important even than this, however, is the fact that MacDiarmid's poetry has become increasingly abstract, cerebral, theoretic, and remote from the basic human sympathies, quite apart from its excessive over-documentation. And yet the overall architectonic, when it shows through, is one of quite remarkable grandeur. And, too, there are many magnificent individual passages in all his longer poems, of which this is only one example. MacDiarmid introduces it in *Lucky Poet* in these words:

'As I have said, I almost always bring the matter of my poetry home to Scotland, and one of the principal elements in my view of life is expressed in these lines:

"It requires great love of it deeply to read
The configuration of a land,

Gradually grow conscious of fine shadings,
Of great meanings in slight symbols,
Hear at last the great voice that speaks softly,
See the swell and fall upon the flank
Of a statue carved out in a whole country's marble,
Be like spring, like a hand in a window
Moving New and Old things carefully to and fro,
Moving a fraction of flower here,
Placing an inch of air there,
And without breaking anything.

So I have gathered unto myself
All the loose ends of Scotland,
And by naming them and accepting them,
Loving them and identifying myself with them,
Attempt to express the whole."

Here, surely, he does succeed in achieving an admirable
balance between intellect and emotion, beauty and power.

1st

novels

viz: Isabel Colegate   The Blackmailer
Man of Power
The Great Occasion

Simon Raven   Feathers of Death
Brother Cain
Doctors Wear Scarlet

David Benedictus   The Fourth of June

Anthony Blond Limited
56 Doughty Street, London W.C.1.

the young writer in scotland

by EDWIN MORGAN

Edwin Morgan is a Lecturer in the Department of English of the University of Glasgow. He is also a poet and translator of Italian and Russian verse.

When I was asked to write about the 'problems facing the young Scottish writer today', I thought it would not be at all hard to enumerate them. Yet the problems are partly those that face young writers everywhere, and if I describe others which are peculiar to Scotland I don't imply that we have any monopoly of heart-searching or frustration. Far from it, indeed; and one of the criticisms Scottish writers might make of themselves is that they have not been sufficientlyaware of the devotion and integrity and commitment which are forced on their contemporaries in more difficult environments—in Spain, Poland, Turkey, Hungary, South Africa, Algeria. When acid tests are no longer applied, either by the merciless hand of life or by authors who take to themselves the lessons imaginative sympathy has to teach them, provincialism with its attendant ills is never far away. This is something we in Scotland have not entirely escaped, and it is as well to recognise the fact, since it leaves its mark on the national life as a whole. Our excuse is that our traditions have given us a good deal of respect for 'provincial' material, but we have been slow to realise that to use such material today the writer must have a broad as well as a narrow view, must be able to think as well as feel. History will sigh with relief when it has finally dragged or cajoled our reluctant, suspicious, complaining country into the second half of the twentieth century!

But to be fair, we have our difficulties. These are partly practical—shortage of literary periodicals, Scottish publishers' lack of interest in Scottish writing—and partly they grow out of the less tangible but very real problems of our relation to traditions, language, and audience.

To deal first with the former: what Scotland needs, and will surely get before long, is a regular monthly literary magazine which will be seriously and professionally produced and will contain not only 'creative' literature (in poetry and fiction) but a critical literature of ideas, a fresh lively current of discussion reaching out into other branches of human activity. Although genius will go its own ways, we have suffered a good deal at the general working level of our literature through the drying-up of almost all our outlets of serious discussion of ideas; and for this, the bitter correspondence-column flytings so typical of Scotland resort too much to personalities to be a useful substitute: in fact they do positive harm, by suggesting to an entertained public that great issues have been aired and examined, which of course by any standards of reason and truth they have not. Another bad result of the gap we have at the moment between the daily newspaper and the quarterly magazine—a gap which the monthly *Scottish Field*, *Scotland's Magazine*, and *Scotland* can fill only to a limited extent because of their other preoccupations—is that comment, whether informative or critical, on current literary and cultural happenings within Scotland is frustrated at every point. There are people in Scotland quite as competent to write on cultural affairs as the majority of those who cover London (and occasionally even 'the provinces') in the pages of the *Spectator* and *New Statesman*, the *Observer* and the *Sunday Times*, yet the would-be Scottish critic or reviewer rarely has the chance of saying what he has to say when he wants to say it. Cultural events in Scotland tend to drift past like a gesticulating frieze which never quite engages with those who sense they are being waved at. And at another level, there is a real need for a journal which would be a general organ of the Scottish universities and include articles on a wide range of intellectual topics. The publication time-lag in most academic and semi-academic journals is now so discouraging that there would be ample room for a journal where less specialised (but rigorously written) essays could find a home and an intelligent public. Both the writers and (I believe) the readers exist in Scotland for such a magazine.

I have stressed, so far, the critical rather than the creative, since there can be no doubt that it is badly needed. It is needed not only to furnish a better, more knowledgeable range of opinion in Scotland, but also to help creative writers themselves, who out of ignorance are sometimes fighting shadows, discovering what has long been known, or clinging manfully to traditions which have now no relevance. We have only ourselves to blame if we allow this situation to continue. We want to see the issues of our time submitted to young and vigorous pens. This, however, leads me to my second group of 'difficulties'.

Scotland is a country in some respects but not in others. It is allowed to be one geographically but not politically, spiritually but not economically. Its people speak in a variety of ways from Southern Standard and Scots-accented English to a fairly well-preserved Scots in some areas, with every possible admixture and often (in the cities) with a very unstable pronunciation. Add to this the separate language-world of Gaelic (though English has made its inroads there too) and you have a picture which still resists, no doubt less strongly each decade, the tempting simplification of 'It's English we speak in Scotland now'. Because the language situation is far from being tidy or clearcut, I feel that the extreme positions of pro-Scots held by Tom Scott and anti-Scots held by W. Price Turner are not the best general guides. When Mr. Scott speaks of English as a mere lingua franca which 'does for non-creative purposes* and is es-

sentially a prose medium', he is brushing aside evidence to the contrary which could easily be set before him—could be taken indeed from Hugh MacDiarmid himself. It is unrealistic to try to persuade oneself that Scots poets cannot now write good poetry in English. But what sort of English? This is where I would part company with those who say 'English English, of course' and leave it at that. Although I want to see—and do see—Scottish writers working on a straightforward Standard English basis, I would also like to see more experiments towards a 'Scotch English' which would move, paradoxically enough, in the two directions of more truthful naturalism and freer manipulation, but in both cases with the aim of infusing a new vitality into the 'English' language, as American and some West Indian and African writers have done in recent years. We have rather neglected the importance of the speech basis ('the current language heightened', in Hopkins's phrase) in the excitement of developing an eclectic or synthetic Scots. Certainly poetry can be written in synthetic Scots, but at the cost of some hypertrophy and imbalance. When Hugh MacDiarmid says that 'any language, real or artificial, serves if a creative artist finds his medium in it', this is a correct, but rather ruthless, poet-centred defence of the method. As we want, at the present time, particularly to encourage the prose literary forms, which we are using too diffidently and unstylishly, we could do with a more open, flexible, yet realistic approach to the whole writer/audience relationship. For the young writer especially, these are not days for being doctrinaire. The dancer Nureyev spoke for many when he said (*Observer*, 3 June 1961):

> Far from becoming fixed, I am striving as hard as I can to find new possibilities, to develop new sides of my nature—even to discover what that nature is. . . . I felt the compulsion to break out of the hard shell, to explore, to test, to grope. . . . I do not want to be told where my proper future lies, what is the 'right' way to develop. I shall try to find this out for myself.

It may be more important for the young writer to realise that the ear is catching up with the eye than that English is

* Notice, in passing, the assumption that 'prose' is 'non-creative'. No wonder the novel is the most backward literary form in Scot-

land! Hugh MacDiarmid also has persistently undervalued the novel as an art form.

displacing Scots or Gaelic. The poem is jumping off the printed page into the gramophone record and the concert hall, and with it goes the poet. Performance—the poet's voice—becomes significant instead of being a mere curiosity. The concept of a living and reacting audience revives. Qualities weakened for centuries—vibrance and warmth, immediacy, tonal indication, subtlety of emphasis—are being regained. Much of the success of recent drama too—in Williams and Miller, in Beckett and Pinter and Osborne—is owed to its 'speaking' vigour and convincingness, its immediate aural impact; as in poetry, this is life entering again through the ear. Successful poetry-readings have been held in Edinburgh and Glasgow, but we are still at a disadvantage, and have a lot of ground to make up, in our poorly developed means of wider communication. Where are the gramophone records of Scottish poets reading their own work? What George Hartley has done in Yorkshire (with his excellent records of William Empson, Philip Larkin, Donald Davie, Thom Gunn, Kingsley Amis), surely someone can emulate in Scotland? The success of the rather specialised Gaelic recording company, Gaelfonn, suggests that there is a market for native products, and as far as poetry is concerned that market need not be confined to Scotland.

How is it that with so many clear and obvious practical difficulties to settle—difficulties 'merely' of publishing, recording, communicating, eliciting public response—Scottish writers continue to frustrate themselves in other and deeper ways? There is no doubt that our literature as a whole, but particularly in the novel and the drama, is like nothing so much as an anxious pedestrian swithering at the end of a zebra crossing: he cannot cross, he cannot cross!—he is afraid he will be swept away by wicked French anti-novelists, run down by noisy Beats, sprung at by Red Cats, lobbed into a dustbin by Joyce's secretary, and if he ever should get to the other side, be served chips with everything. Oh no, he can't, he mustn't! And yet he must. This has to be gone through, this has to be crossed. In literature, as also perhaps in education, business, and industry, spectres have to be laid, eyes have to be raised, admissions have to be made, quarrels have to be compounded, the rest of the world must be admitted to exist. And I am thinking not simply of creative methods, important as these are, but even more of the creative spirit, the spirit of the times which seems alien only to those who cannot see how dangerously conservative and tradition-minded Scotland has become. Anyone who thinks I am asking for Robin Jenkins to write like Robbe-Grillet or Iain Crichton Smith to write like Ginsberg misunderstands an essential point. What matters is that the achievements and purposes of contemporary European and American writing should be known in Scotland—known and discussed, not necessarily imitated. It would be surprising if they failed to act as a stimulus—even a stimulus to 'admire and do otherwise'—but the main thing is simply to get our country to break out from its prickly isolation and have the self-confidence to measure its creative life against the best and vividest examples from outside. Many young writers in the past have felt that it was impossible to do this and at the same time remain in Scotland, with all the demands living in Scotland makes on one's becoming a 'Scottish writer'. There is something wrong with the literary society which cannot keep a W. S. Graham, an Ian Dallas, an Alexander Trocchi, all of whom in very different ways might have contributed essences and advances their country was badly in need of. I believe this situation is changing; the new generation of writers is more willing to give Scotland a try, and to feel able to place what is national and specific against the huge but not daunting backcloth of the world even Scotsmen must live in. Let them travel: I hope they will; but then let them return. Not, I hope, to the atmosphere described by Margaret Tait:

Only in Scotland
Do those who love you kick you in the face.
They do it on purpose.
They feel they have to.
They feel they must
—For a valuable lesson, so they believe.
But we don't need the lesson.
We'd rather those who loved us just loved us.
We don't need the kicking in the face.

This is the last problem of the young Scottish writer—how to overcome opposition or neglect without falling into that bitterness which has sapped the strength of so many. This is partly economics (more could be done to help the young writer when he is at the most crucial stage—all but the most granite-minded need a minimal encouragement just to continue); partly education (to dissolve in the public the remnants of a philistine/moralistic distrust of the arts); and partly it is the writer's own attitude to his fellow-men, which has often been so uncomfortable, so touchy, so un-sympathetic. One must believe that sympathy and help and goodwill are at least as necessary as flytings and bonny fechters, and in our present age these qualities shine across frontiers. The new generation has to build rather than to divide. What better place to do it than this place where it is so difficult: Scotland.

DOMI MINA
NUS TIO
ILLU MEA

The Novelist as Philosopher

Studies in French Fiction 1935–1960

EDITED BY JOHN CRUICKSHANK

The authors of this symposium have been left free to express their personal views and indulge in their private enthusiasms, thus making possible variety and liveliness within a general framework. The novelists discussed include Camus, Beckett, Sartre, Robbe-Grillet and Simone de Beauvoir.   21s net

OXFORD UNIVERSITY PRESS

day three : **commitment**

The topic for discussion on the Third Day
of the Conference is Commitment.
Perhaps associated most strongly with the
dedication of so many artists and
intellectuals in Europe and America
during the nineteen-thirties to leftist
political ideals, 'commitment' as a general
principle for the novelist to accept or
reject remains a live issue. Raymond
Williams, who regards himself as a
committed writer, here explains what he
understands by the description, while
Alain Robbe-Grillet argues that a writer
can only be committed to his art. Dwight
Macdonald comments briefly from an
American point of view; and Andrew
Hook writes on commitment in terms of
the continuing aesthetic problem of the
relationship between the individual and
society.

Only a few months old, COLLIER BOOKS have become the most significant new line of quality paperbacks in a generation

Send for this

Catalogue now

and see why

commitment

by RAYMOND WILLIAMS

Raymond Williams is University Lecturer in English and Fellow of Jesus College, Cambridge. His publications include a novel, 'Border Country' (1960), and two studies of cultural history and ideas, 'Culture and Society' (1958), and 'The Long Revolution' (1961).

It is nobody's business to lay down general rules for writers. When a government or party does so, in an attempt to exact general commitment to a particular cause, it is acting according to the habits of governments and parties, which we have been well trained to recognise and which many of us are in a good position to resist. Yet the attempt to lay down general rules is not made only by governments and parties. It is made also, and especially today in the North Atlantic area, by fashion and by critics. Most critics are at least a generation out of date, as far as original work in the arts is concerned, and fashion, following them, is usually set in complacencies of attitude and phrase which were young with our fathers. The current argument about commitment, in England and similar countries, is not about real issues at all. The ordinary proposition, of commitment and service to a cause, dates from the nineteen-thirties, but what is not so often recognised is that the ordinary opposition to commitment—the phrases and arguments usually deployed —dates also from the nineteen-thirties and indeed from even earlier. Unless we can get free of this combination of archaism and complacency we shall not be able to discuss, with any success, the real and living issues to which commitment, as an idea, still points. Certainly we have to resist the continued pressure of governments and parties. But also we have to resist fashion, which is equally deadly. Indeed fashion, in the market democracies, plays a very similar rôle to that of governments and parties in non-democratic societies. Fashion seeks to impose rules, using its alternatives of success or ridicule with its own kind of arbitrariness. For what are we to say when fashion, in the name of the freedom of the artist, insists that commitment is not his business ? Who then is making the general rules ? The extraordinary arrogance of this kind of interdiction, this inflation of a personal preference into a general and absolute case, will not fail to be recognised as arbitrary, however striking its liberal rhetoric. Like other kinds of liberal rhetoric, the essential proposition behind the assertion of freedom is the setting of limits to what manner of thing freedom is. Men are not to be free in ways other than those defined in the special proposition of freedom. Artists ought not to be committed, because the position of the artist ought not to be regulated by anyone. These essentially absurd positions, however widely syndicated, simply have to be rejected, if the matter is to be seriously discussed at all.

I regard myself as a committed writer, and I want to try to explain what I understand as commitment. In my novels and in my general writings (with differences, evidently, corresponding to the differences of form) I regard myself as committed to a particular theme, which in fact, outside literature, is also a way of looking at the world, of living in it and indeed seeking to change it. I was committed to this theme by nobody but myself, yet the very form of this statement is an aspect of the theme. For indeed, in quite real ways, I was committed to this theme by my history, which in its turn is not the history of one man only but of very many people. Yet it has not been a case of simply accepting the pressure, accommodating myself to the precast mould, of this history. That, indeed, would not be commitment at all; it would be merely inheritance. The commitment began as I began to be conscious of this history, and in that sense transcends it. I was not able to write my novel *Border Country* until I was sufficiently conscious, both of myself and of the shaping history, to be able to go beyond it into a work which was a record of neither but rather a creation, a valuing creation, of both. In the same way I was not able to write of the tradition which *Culture and Society* embodies until I had reached the point where I was beyond the tradition and in a position to try to extend it. The exploration of experience, until those decisive moments, was in no way committed. The commitment came when I was conscious enough to value and to choose. I might add that I did not experience this decision as a loss of freedom, but in fact, deeply, as a first step towards it. The commitment, when it came, was not final yet was quite precise: a particular conviction of identity, as a person and as a writer. If this conviction (as some critics have said) is also the definition of a cause—that is to say, if its roots and directions are shared by others—then of course I am glad.

It is not easy, in polemic, to define or re-define a theme which has in fact been embodied in books. Yet I must attempt a brief description, in order to mark off what I have been saying from other ideas of commitment, and, more urgently, to mark my rejection of the state of mind and feeling which finds commitment irrelevant (not merely, as I have said, for itself, but for the world).

I believe that in the novel and in politics alike we are crippled by a deep and blind division between personal and social reality. The assumption that these are separate areas of experience is bad enough. The further assumption, that in the act of writing a man must choose between these areas, and in the choice declare himself poet or sociologist, is in my view disastrous. If we select from the range of our experience two sovereign areas, which we go on to label as 'individual' and 'society', we are unlikely to be able to understand either societies or individuals. We shall get, while we rest in this division, on the one hand a sociology and a politics which have no place for persons but only for collective modes; on the other hand a literature which either artificially limits its scale of human reference (in ways that earlier literatures would find absurd) or which in the very quest for persons ends by rejecting persons (only it calls this rejection a rejection of sociology or politics). Once the separate sovereign areas are set, the habits of each play into

the hands of the other, and conflict between them—a complacent, boring, and destructive conflict—seems inevitable. Of course this conflict both reflects and makes actual history, actual experience. The structures of totalitarian and market societies alike depend on a reduction of individuals to collective modes, to be controlled by a party or administered by the market and its highly developed methods of research and communication. Within such societies, the personal revolt is inevitable, but again and again it takes the form, whether in literature or in social thinking, of a revolt against what is called 'the mass', which is only finally identifiable, in this kind of thinking, as other persons. The personal revolt against the 'herd' or the 'crowd' is commonplace, but it is also self-defeating. In the name of 'the person' we can become indifferent or hostile to others, as in one significantly popular kind of contemporary novel. But then, as the indifference and hostility become set, as this version and expectation of others become normal, the defence of 'the person' becomes more and more impossible, for in the act of what we describe as defence we are creating a world in which the acceptance of others, in any full human sense, is difficult and indeed dangerous. Nor is this a world which can be reformed by any ordinary social or political action, by work on the collective modes. Life can only move again, between individuals and societies, when we are pressed by experience to the nature of the separation itself, the inherited and false separation between psychological and social reality.

My own work as a writer is the exploration of this separation, and of the roads across and beyond it. My commitment is to a particular unity of experience, which I have both known and must seek to create. The separation is now so deep that no single writer can bridge and go beyond it. I try to listen to all the voices I can, whether defeated by this gulf or still struggling—as I believe many now are—to cross it, to make communication. With many writers whom I do not personally know, I feel a comradeship of struggle which yet commits none of us to anything beyond this struggle itself: certainly no commitment to anything outside and distinguishable from ourselves, though in fact it is necessarily a commitment of ourselves to others; of ourselves as ourselves to others, for that is society, as it is also personal relationship of any active kind. It feels as much like exposure as commitment: a total exposure, as man and writer, to the actual range of experience, without the defensive or protective devices of the split in consciousness. What begins in the process of exposure to a whole reality can end as involvement in it, in active ways. By commitment we have usually meant the latter, and this is right if we can come

to it as ourselves. But the commitment that now matters, as I see it, is the first stage, the exposure, the commitment to exposure. For in this we break down the false choice, between person and society, which has cursed both persons and societies. We break down also, if we can find the strength in ourselves, the choice between the consequent versions of 'poet' and 'sociologist', whether as men or as novelists. There is neither regulation, nor the regulation of indifference, but as in art of any kind a personal vision which may become a common vision.

the writer's only commitment is to literature

by ALAIN ROBBE-GRILLET

Robbe-Grillet is a leading exponent of the French 'nouveau roman'

Has life a meaning? What meaning? What is man's place in the world? One can easily see why the objects Balzac was fond of describing were so reassuring; they belonged to a world in which man was the master; they were simply articles or property, with no other purpose than to be possessed, retained, or acquired. The identity between the object and its owner was complete: a waistcoat was not merely a waistcoat, it was a trait of character, and at the same time a social position. The reason for all things was to be found in man; he was the key to the universe and its natural master, as of divine right.

Very little of all this is still valid today. While the middle classes were gradually ceasing to fulfil their rôle and forfeiting their prerogatives, thought was seeking its foundation elsewhere than in essence, the field of philosophic research was steadily being invaded by phenomenology, the physical sciences were discovering the realm of discontinuity, and psychology itself was undergoing parallel changes which were no less complete.

The meaning of the world around us can no longer be considered as other than fragmentary, temporary, and even contradictory, and is always in dispute. How can a work of art set out to illustrate any sort of meaning which is known in advance? The modern novel is an enquiry, but an enquiry which creates its own meaning as it goes along. Has reality a meaning? The contemporary artist cannot reply; he does not know the answer. All he can say is that the reality may acquire a meaning through his work, and only after that work is completed.

Why should this conception be regarded as pessimistic?

At all events it is diametrically opposed to surrender. We can no longer believe in the fixed, unyielding realities provided for us, first of all by a divine order of things, and then by the rationalistic order of the nineteenth century. All our hope is founded on man: it is only through the forms created by him that meaning can be brought into the world.

dwight macdonald of 'the new yorker' wrote:

'The question of "commitment" was settled for me in the thirties when we on Partisan Review *struggled against the Communists, who were trying to slip that particular strait-jacket over American poets, novelists and critics. Since they didn't have state power, they failed. I also remember M. Sartre's sophisticated absurdities on the subject. The issue has been settled a long time ago and that the English should still be kicking it around is an interesting example of cultural lag.'*

commitment and reality

by ANDREW HOOK

Andrew Hook is a member of the Department of English of the University of Edinburgh.

While his *Crack-Up* articles, which tried to account for an overwhelming sense of personal frustration and failure, were appearing in *Esquire*, Scott Fitzgerald received a letter from his friend Dos Passos of which this is part:

I've been wanting to see you, naturally, to argue about your *Esquire* articles—Christ man, how do you find time in the middle of the general conflagration to worry about all that stuff? . . . After all not many people write as well as you do. Here you've gone and spent forty years in perfecting an elegant and complicated piece of machinery (tool I was going to say) and the next forty years is the time to use it—or as long as the murderous forces of history will let you.

The date is 1936 and this is the letter of a committed writer to one he regards as uncommitted. Dos Passos cannot understand why at this critical moment of time Fitzgerald should allow himself to be so taken up with personal, individual problems and concerns. As an artist he should be preoccupied not with the cracking-up of his own life, but with what Dos Passos recognises as the imminent dissolution and disintegration of the society and world of which he is part. For Dos Passos the duty of the writer is not to look inward, to the exploration of the individual consciousness, but outward to society at large, to the broader forces and movements which mould and control man's destiny. The final confrontation is not that of man and his deepest, truest, thinking and feeling self, but that of man and 'the murder-ous forces of history'. Just such an argument as this over the necessary priority of either the inner, psychological reality, or the outer, social reality lies behind every debate on commitment.

Dos Passos' last phrase, however,—the murderous forces of history—provides us with a clue to the origins of commitment as an ideal for the writer. Commitment, as it is generally understood—the acceptance by the writer of an extra-artistic, usually political, programme of action and belief which lies behind his creative endeavours—depends essentially on a Romantic view of society, of what society stands for. In the eighteenth century in England, writers such as Pope and Swift were just as much committed, committed to a dream, a vision of the ideal society, as any of the English or French or American writers of the nineteen-thirties. But their dream was the dream of all of their society; their vision was a vision to which all reasonable men gave their consent—hence the power with which they assailed the non-ideal elements in their society. This typical Augustan situation, however, in which individual values reflected social values, in which the individual found the values in which he believed endorsed and upheld by the society of which he was part, was not an enduring one. Whether it had ever in fact been more than a literary reality may be open to question. But the point is that the development of Romanticism meant it ceased even to be that. One of the manifold meanings of Romanticism is precisely a new interest in the individual as individual rather than as member of society, a turning away from society to the individual as the focus of interest, the centre of consciousness. The consequence was that social and individual values tended to diverge. And for the Romantic artist, as for a great many other artists and writers down to the present day, society came to be seen not as the institutionalised defender and protector of humane values, of 'the good life', but as a vast, imponderable, unregenerate mass, destructive of everything the good life embodies.

Where the Augustan artist is typically the spokesman for, the defender of, the ideals of his society, the Romantic

45

artist is again and again the defender of ideals to which he feels his society is hostile. Seeing society in this light, as something by definition destructive of individual values, how could the post-Augustan writer respond? How could he preserve and defend those values in which he believed? One method was that of strategic withdrawal. The artist embraced his alienation from society, defined himself as artist precisely by that alienation, and proclaimed the absolute autonomy of art and artistic values. The other was the method of counter-attack, by which the artist provided society with images of its own repressiveness and destructiveness, and by so doing implicitly or explicitly pointed the way to social reformation.

It has already been noted that Romanticism involved a new interest in the individual—in the individual and his personal response to experience; a cultivation then of the feelings, of the individual sensibility. But the question of the relationship between the individual response and the established, impersonal, social realities, between what might be called the private and public visions of reality, is at once problematical. The artist who pursues the first of the methods mentioned above—the method that may produce the doctrine of art for art's sake—unhesitatingly follows his private vision to the total disregard of any kind of public reality. He is committed, in other words, to the cultivation of the self, the individual sensibility. The artist who follows the second way—the prototype of what we understand by the committed writer—also pursues a private vision; only to realise it he becomes preoccupied with the external, social reality. Neither method, that is, successfully overcomes the difficulty of relating the private and public worlds, the inner world of private sensibility and the outer world of social reality.

Jane Austen was probably the last English writer for whom these two worlds could be readily reconciled—and of course Jane Austen looks back to the eighteenth century rather than on to the nineteenth. Certainly the work of her contemporaries and successors manifests no such harmonious reconciliation; rather have private sensibility and public reality remained firmly opposed to each other. Once the personal response to experience was allowed superior validity, perhaps such an opposition followed inevitably; certainly once the artistic effort itself came to be identified wholly with the cultivation of the individual sensibility, once the private vision came to be equated with the life of the imagination, then reconciliation was problematical indeed.

But for the majority of Victorian writers an unheeding pursuit of the private vision, at the expense of the surrounding social reality, was never even a possibility. Most of the Victorians were all too aware of that social reality with its orthodoxies of conduct and beliefs, established and sanctioned by custom, tradition, and even religion. For most of the Victorians society represented a reality that could not be denied or ignored, towards which the artist as man, and probably as artist too, owed certain responsibilities, certain duties. It is, in fact, the recognition and acceptance of these duties and responsibilities which create the 'divided self' of the typical Victorian artist, drawn by both the public and private worlds. The Victorian artist comes more and more to identify the sources of his creative inspiration with something that is private and individual, something entirely detached from the normal, social world, something which may even be inimical to that everyday world of moral choices and responsibilities. Carried to an extreme, this identification of the sources of creative inspiration with something dangerously private and non-moral, brings the artist to a basic mistrust of the imagination itself, to the belief that the palace of art may be a lotos island, a seduction from the real world of essential moral responsibility. Wordsworth, Tennyson, Arnold, Charlotte Brontë, George Eliot, George Meredith—all of them were aware of such a danger. And surely it is feelings of a similar kind about the status of the imaginative process which underlie most of the modern arguments in favour of commitment.

But 'duty'—the escape route from the self—which we may fairly see as the Victorian version of 'commitment', did not prove itself a powerful, creative stimulus. The careers of, say, Wordsworth and Tennyson rather suggest the reverse. 'Duty', seen as something opposed to the cultivation, or indulgence, of the individual sensibility, seems to have had a deadening effect upon that sensibility, that is, upon the springs of creative expression. Only when the conflict between the private and public worlds was raised to the level of a dialogue between 'duty' and the 'self' did any kind of imaginative release follow—as novels such as *Jane Eyre*, *The Mill on the Floss*, and *The Ordeal of Richard Feverel* suggest.

The doctrine of the essentially private and individual nature of the aesthetic response to experience, and of the autonomy of that response, was one that survived unscathed in the literary revolution that occurred early in this century. Hence the choice for the modern writer between commitment and non-commitment is essentially the same choice as his Victorian predecessor made between duty and the self. No doubt, of course, the choice is often not a fully conscious one, and no doubt, too, most writers would be unwilling to accept either of the extreme positions advocated by its partisans. Certainly few of the great writers of the twentieth century have been prepared to accept the logic of art for art's sake; but few too, it seems to me, have been prepared to accept engagement with the external, social reality as the only kind of engagement that matters. To do so would amount to a denial of the validity of the individual, feeling response—which remains identified with the sources of the creative process itself.

The example of those writers who have accepted the ideal of commitment certainly does not suggest that commitment necessarily produces any kind of creative sterility. But commitment does tend in practice to mean the rejection of whole areas of human experience—areas accessible only through the exercise of the individual sensibility. If over-cultivation of the private sensibility leads to narrowness, limitation, and finally to a self-indulgent turning away from the external world altogether, commitment can lead to undesirable limitations of a different kind—limitations in kinds of subject-matter and in methods of rendering experience. The committed writer tends to over-simplify; to see human experience only in terms of the pattern to which he is committed. This is perhaps the greatest weakness of all committed, social realist writing; the individual is seen as the helpless victim of the murderous forces of history and society, and as such he ceases to be an individual. In *The Grapes of Wrath*, for example, the members of the Joad family are intended to be representative of an under-privileged and exploited section of American society. But their representative nature—the sense in which they illustrate the pattern—seems in some typical way to act against their full imaginative realisation.

But the work of John Dos Passos himself provides us with a perfect symbol of the basic difficulty confronting the writer preoccupied with the nature of the external, social reality. *USA*, Dos Passos' trilogy about American society, greatly under-rated by current fashions, is of course in the main dedicated to that reality. But Dos Passos is impelled to admit into this public world, the other private, passional world of the individual sensibility: hence the recurring device of the Camera Eye which renders the individual response to experience.

Dos Passos' instinct that the private and public visions of the individual and society must be combined is clearly a sound one. And one may go on believing that some kind of reconciliation can be obtained irrespective of whether one begins with Dos Passos' 'murderous forces of history' or with Fitzgerald's exploration of the individual consciousness.

olympia

a literary
review
from
the publishers
who
do not
accept
censorship

OLYMPIA PRESS

7 Rue St Séverin

Paris 5

OLYMPIA is a new monthly review from Paris, published by Olympia Press, the most important firm of Paris publishers publishing in English, who first brought out such masterpieces of contemporary literature as Samuel Beckett's Malloy, Burrough's The Naked Lunch, Nabokov's Lolita, Lawrence Durrell's Black Book, Henry Miller's Plexus, as well as countless other titles, many of them still not publishable in anglo-saxon countries. Olympia Press has always been in the forefront of the fight against censorship, believing that in a free society writers should be free to write what they want and the public to read what it wants. Now they are publishing a monthly magazine which is available by direct postal subscription from Paris. The first issues have contained stories, extracts from new novels, poetry and articles by such authors as Lawrence Durrell, Jock Carroll, William Burroughs, J. P. Donleavy, Maxwell Kenton, and other well-known authors. There is a monthly $1000 short story contest, and the magazine, which is well-produced in a luxurious format, contains several striking photographic features in each issue. In the first two numbers for instance were highly unusual features on Paris 'clochards', on chastity belts—from medieval models to those designed in this century, on the Templars, and on erotic Paris postcards of the turn of the century.

day four : censorship

On its Fourth Day the Conference will
take up the many-sided and difficult
problem of censorship in its various
personal, social, political, and legal
aspects. To indicate some of the difficulties
involved two writers were invited to
contribute articles written from quite
different points of view: Denis Donoghue
was asked to survey the problem of
censorship from a general, objective
standpoint, while Colin MacInnes was
invited to comment more from the point
of view of the individual writer. The
articles which follow constitute their
replies.

eight propositions on censorship

by DENIS DONOGHUE

Dr. Donoghue is a Lecturer in English at University College, Dublin. His book, 'The Third Voice: Modern British and American Verse Drama', appeared in 1959, and he is a regular contributor to British and American literary journals.

1. *The entire subject is distasteful*

By which I refer to the enormous possibilities of resentment, humiliation, righteousness, as the 'I' strives to be holier-than-Thou while grasping all the forensic advantages. Even to see the word on a page is to bristle with anticipations of distress. We automatically respond to the word as if it conjured the world of Kafka's parables, down to the last unanswered question: such are its connotations, alas. The Freedom of the Self; moral responsibility; these are on trial, if not already condemned. It is difficult to be civil and gracious in these conditions.

2. *But we should not assume too readily that Freedom challenged is Freedom lost*

It may be the means of defining a term badly in need of definition. In any event our automatic response to the word must be questioned. G. H. Mead, the first of many citations: 'The essential characteristic of intelligent behaviour is delayed responses—a halt in behaviour while thinking is going on'. If—Mead again—the Self is developed through the assumption of rôles and one of these is the rôle of critic, hence in an intelligent life the basic pattern, far from being 'free', is already self-restrictive. 'The immediate effect of such rôle-taking lies in the control which the individual is able to exercise over his own response.' Without this faculty, we should probably find all forms of law—traffic regulations, dogma, time-tables—quite intolerable. A footnote in Mead refers to Freud's conception of the psychological 'censor' as a partial recognition of this operation of social control in terms of *self*-criticism. Hence the notion of a potentially 'free' Self fighting for its life against a murderous Society whose weapons are law, prosecution, and censorship is already inaccurate. We are censoring ourselves all the time.

3. *The challenge should be met by setting up the conditions in which an equable discussion may proceed*

The imagery of war is out of place. Most discussions of Censorship are vitiated by the assumptions under which they are conducted; 'Artist' versus 'Philistine'; 'Anarchist' versus 'Patriot'. Mead is again relevant: if thought is a 'conversation' with a listener-speaker whom each of us invents in all goodwill, we should be able to meet 'real' disputants in equally generous encounters. Our images should be civic, communicative, fusive: these are the auspices under which we may—must—concern ourselves with the relation between books, magazines, films, advertisements, slogans, and—the result of a thousand different forces—the 'quality' of our lives. The case of *Lady Chatterley's Lover* was journalistically interpreted as the victory of the Individual and the defeat of Authority: it could have been interpreted with greater civility as the mediation of a topically defined Law, a new synthesis of co-operative energies.

4. *Censorship is not an aesthetic act*

Even if in Britain and the United States the aesthetic quality of a book is now deemed to be legally admissible. The final decision in censorship is not in the hands of artists or critics; it is given by those whose province is action rather than appreciation or contemplation. This is a proper delegation of concern. One of the happiest developments in modern democratic law is the realisation that even in the province of action it is possible to discriminate effectively between *Ulysses* and *Hot Dames on Cold Slabs*.

5. *Censorship is an act of politics or jurisprudence*

And therefore *in principle* it needs no more defence than any other act of politics or jurisprudence; it refers to the duty of the State in maintaining public order, including what Lord Radcliffe calls 'the old aedile business of keeping the roads clean and the air sweet'. There is no more objection to Censorship *in principle* than to the authority of a Society or a Church which prescribes rules for the conduct of its members.

6. *Conversations between Art and Politics should be sponsored with all available goodwill*

In democratic countries the signs are now more favourable than they have been for many years. In regard to the censorship of books, the present tendency of politicians and jurists is to give primary consideration to the author's presumed intention—as disclosed by the nature of the book itself—rather than to the possible or probable effects of his book upon an anonymous reader of uncertain age, temperament, and mental condition. This is due to the common acknowledgement that a necessary relation between a criminal's acts and his reading habits has not yet been shown; most students of behaviour agree that crime is the result of many factors, of which the criminal's reading habits are probably of marginal importance; the question is still wide open. In the meantime the presumed intention of the author is a more reliable factor in discrimination. If conversations between Art and Politics issue in the acknowledgement of a difference between the intentions of James Joyce and those of 'Hank Janson', and if this effects a corresponding discrimination in decisions involving the province of action, this is a happy mediation, and there is hope.

7. *Censorship is a problem in direct proportion to the failure of Education*

(A terrifying theme, for which I can offer here only a few chapter-titles. Universal Literacy and the 'New Illiteracy'; see R. P. Blackmur's *The Lion and the Honeycomb* for the problem and its attendant fears. Education as Technique or Method. The Lowering of Standards in favour of the Many; see Hannah Arendt's *Between Past and Future*. The Corrosion of Value. The Conspiracy to sever Fact and Value and to imply that the former is the sole medium of Education. Quantity, not Quality.)

But Education is a long-term answer. Even if Periclean habits of discrimination were to be developed all over the world in the year A.D. 2040 the achievement would arrive too late for the millions who now read the comics in firm preference to Dante. In the meantime no one really knows what forms the education of the young should take in a mass society. But—to return to the jurists—it is probably a sound instinct to hand over the protection of the young, in the field of mass culture, to their parents: I assume that this is one of the effects of the 'intentionalist' focus in juridical censorship; a parent should be the first to show concern for the 'quality' of his child's life.

8 *The greatest danger facing a writer from the direction of Censorship is not that he will be silenced, but that by meeting force with force he will undermine his own imagination*

Three points: (*a*) The function of the artist remains what it has always been, to propose a reasoned human image, to liberate the powers of the rational imagination. The artist must not allow any force to eject him from the 'centrality', the sanity, of his own rôle; he must not yield to the disintegration, the mindlessness, of his time; he must not allow himself to be driven into the hysteria of imagination, into vertigo or conceit. His special power is intelligence, imagination, the rational imagination: he is at home in no other realm.

(*b*) In the conversations between Art and Politics the greatest present happiness is that in democratic countries there is a growing acknowledgement that Art is in some undefined sense autonomous; that a serious image of human life has value and authority which Politics should be slow to deny and quick to defend. There is a growing acknowledgement that the orders of politics, law, and economics cannot lay hold of the full human reality, that there are forces and motives which can be apprehended only by the rational imagination. The function of the artist in the realm of action is silently to remind Authority that this is so.

(*c*) Kenneth Burke used to say that the motto of the Imagination is—when in Rome do as the Greeks. But this would be a dangerous prescription in totalitarian countries, and I should be slow to require an artist to do what I would not be prepared to do myself. To preserve the gist of truth perhaps we might translate the motto to read—when in Rome speak like a Roman who values Athens; in a Roman artist the rational imagination will 'allow for' an Athenian voice and will speak a correspondingly gracious idiom, thus certifying its own sanity. When Rome 'allows for' Athens, the sound we hear is self-criticism, conversation, communication, dialogue.

THE CLASSICS OF MODERN FICTION

Camus Cary Cocteau Colette Douglas Faulkner Fitzgerald Forster Gide Golding Hemingway Huxley Joyce Kafka Lowry Mann Mauriac Sartre

appear in Penguin Modern Classics

Write to Penguin Books, Harmondsworth, Middlesex for a complete list of books available, including many works by authors attending the International Writers' Conference, Edinburgh, 1962

METHUEN publishers of

JEAN ANOUILH   ISAAC BABEL

KARL BJARNHOF   BERTOLT BRECHT

MICHEL BUTOR   MILOVAN DJILAS

MAX FRISCH   JEAN GIRAUDOUX

ERIH KOŠ   HALLDOR LAXNESS

JEAN-PAUL SARTRE   CARL ZUCKMAYER

METHUEN & Co Ltd 36 ESSEX STREET · STRAND · LONDON WC2

on censorship

by COLIN MacINNES

**Colin MacInnes is known both as a novelist and as an
acute observer of the contemporary British social
scene. His novels include 'City of Spades', 'Absolute
Beginners', and 'Mr. Love and Justice'. His most
recent book is 'England, Half English' (1961), a collection of essays.**

While plays and films are subject to overt control in our
country, censorship of the printed word is indirect.

Let us first consider books. The initial censor the
writer meets with is his publisher. Few publishers today
suggest cuts or alterations to conform with their personal
sense of what is fitting (as they did, notoriously, in D. H.
Lawrence's day); but they must all remember the laws on
libel and obscenity, which are still severe. The emancipa-
tion resulting from cases like *Regina v.* Penguin Books remains relative, since trials on such a scale are expensive and
time-absorbing; and faced with the choice of persuading a
writer to change a doubtful text, or of risking litigation
after publication, the publisher is likely to take the easier
course.

The two ensuing censorships of books are largely unknown to the general public. The first is by the printers
who, quite naturally wishing to avoid possible subsequent
lawsuits, may refuse to print at all. And this refusal need
not arise merely from their own interpretation of the law,
but—unlike the publishers' reluctance—from questions of

taste: usually not that of the directors of the printing firm,
but of the typographers they employ. (In 1951, two firms
refused to print a book of mine to which their managements
did not object, but to which their Chapel Fathers at the
machines took censorious exception.) As the law blames the
printer as well as the publisher and writer for any statutory
infraction, one cannot really blame the printer for his prud-
ence; since he clearly has not the same moral responsibility
for the material of the book he prints, as have the other
parties involved.

The next censorship of books is by the Libraries, public
and commercial. Their buying-committees are in effect
censors, for if they decide a volume is 'not suitable' for their
readers, they boycott it. (A commercial library which had
taken 200 copies of an earlier book of mine decided, on
grounds unknown to anyone, that it did not approve of its
successor. They bought 6 token copies to show, I suppose,
that they weren't censoring at all.)

Subject to these indirect restrictions, artistic expression in
books is relatively free; and more so, I would say, than in
any other printed medium. There is always, of course, the
possibility of an ill-informed denunciation by some journalist
on the make, but this does not lead to suppression and probably has, in terms of readership, the reverse effect to that
the moralising journalist intended.

When we come to media not yet mentioned—newspapers, magazines, radio and television—though the indirect censorship is greater, its operation is more subtle and
oblique.

To begin with, there is considerable self-censorship by
the writer. You would not offer a laudatory portrait of, say,
Dr. Nkrumah to the *Daily Telegraph*, nor a piece denoun-
cing homosexuality to the *New Statesman*. But even when the
theme seems to the writer to 'fit' the journal to which he
offers it, he will probably trim his sails, to some extent, to
the known policy of the journal. By this I mean not that he
will tell lies, but perhaps not tell the entire truth as he sees
it. For this one cannot altogether blame the editors—though
some allow far greater freedom to writers they respect than

others—since they are responsible to their proprietors for the overall tone of the publication.

So far as the press and periodicals go, I would advance, in the matter of censorship, this axiom. If the writer is original, and his ideas appear startling or subversive, he should seek as his medium a journal of maximum obscurity and of minimum remuneration. In my experience, it is only in journals of 1-2000 circulation, and who pay their writers little and often nothing, that you can place a piece in which you say everything you want to on any really controversial theme.

In radio, the convention (much prized by the B.B.C.) that the Corporation does not censor, is a myth. The reality has often been described (*e.g.* by Henry Fairlie). The producer proposes to you some scintillating theme, or you come up with one yourself. In your early days, you were in astonished admiration at the Corporation's daring; but you soon discover in what, at the 'policy' level, the magic formula consists. It is to discuss on the air the most controversial topics while contriving to rob them of all controversy. The magic is not effected by asking you to alter your script (let alone crudely ordering you to do so), but by making it so evident that dangerous aspects of the theme should be omitted, that you realise you must either refuse to do the job at all, or else tone the whole thing down to an acceptable nullity.

An additional subtlety of the manœuvre is the use the policy people make of the unfortunate producer. He (or she) is usually just as anxious as you are to tell the entire story. But because you like the producer, and know he will be in professional danger if you try to insist on telling the whole truth, you refrain from putting your colleague in an impossible position. As for the policy-makers, they shelter behind the producer and remain prudently invisible. In even the largest newspapers, it's not that hard for a writer to see anyone, up to and including the editor, to argue about policy. At the B.B.C., for whom I've done I suppose some 2000 programmes, I have never met (other than once or twice socially) anyone above producer level; nor, for that matter, have I ever seen administrators descend from their office eyries to the studio floor where the job gets done—or fails to.

With television it is even worse. In the B.B.C. they don't mind overmuch what the public think, provided you can conform, more or less, to their neo-Reithian orthodoxy. In television, while they have not yet evolved their own theology, the public reaction is the essential consideration. This applies just as much to their 'cultural' programmes as to their overtly pop ones. The television companies may imagine that if they envisage, for a 'cultural' programme, a 'low' viewing figure of say two millions, a great concession has been made by commerce to the arts. But in fact, not at all. It cannot be stressed enough that there are innumerable cultural topics which, if truthfully treated, can *never* appeal to more than a minute minority of possibly several tens of thousands; so that to achieve objectivity, an audience of two millions is as inhibiting as one of twenty. The circle the TV companies are trying to square is to give maximum reality to a maximum audience, and this cannot be done without either sacrificing much of the reality, or putting on programmes at prohibitive cost which are bound to repel all but an infinitely small percentage of viewers.

On the whole theme of censorship in our country, I have two final observations. I am totally opposed to it myself, in any form whatever, if only because I believe no one is worthy to decide when it should be enforced. 'Censorship', in operation, is not the abstract principle it may seem: it consists of fallible and usually anonymous men and women making value judgements of immense influence, which they can never be capable, morally, intellectually or socially, of making on this scale. My other reflection is that when considering censorship we are apt—as we are when we consider so many English institutions—to congratulate ourselves and suppose all is for the best, without discovering what is really happening, or thinking how this could be bettered.

day five : the novel and the future

On its Final Day the Conference will discuss the future of the novel. Ever since its birth there have been those prepared to proclaim the imminent death of the novel. Somehow it has gone on flourishing, but today the voices prophesying decline and decay are as loud as ever. To provide a background for this final discussion the following three questions were submitted to a wide range of writers and critics:

a Do you feel that the novel is in danger of losing its place as the dominant literary form—the place commonly allowed it since early last century—that it is in fact a dying literary genre?

b Will the novel continue to develop and is the direction of development discernible?

c Will the development of new formal and stylistic techniques lead to a further loss of audience for the novel?

The pages that follow contain a symposium of answers from ANGUS WILSON, NATHALIE SARRAUTE, KINGSLEY AMIS, PHILIP TOYNBEE, HAROLD NICOLSON, JULIAN MITCHELL, NEIL GUNN, JOHN BRAINE, MURIEL SPARK.

If you stop to make up a list of the most significant contemporary authors, you

will find that a very large proportion are published by the small firm of JOHN CALDER, who have made a speciality of publishing unusual books of very high literary quality. Authors that for years have been known only by small literary coteries are now emerging as the giants of the contemporary scene. Pre-eminent among these is Samuel Beckett, whose three great post-war novels are now available in one large volume. The trilogy contains **Malloy, Malone Dies** *and* **The Unnameable.** *His earlier novels* **Murphy** *and* **Watt** *will shortly be reissued in paperback. We also publish his* **Poems in English.** *Other novelists who have broken through in a major way onto the contemporary British scene are Nathalie Sarraute, whose* **Portrait of a Man Unknown** *and* **The Planetarium** *are recognised as major advances in literature (the term anti-novel was first coined by Sartre for her work), Marguerite Duras, the fiery author of* **Hiroshima, mon amour,** *whose sensitive novels,* **The Square, Little Horses of Tarquinia** *and* **Moderato cantabile,** *have earned her a special place in modern writing, and perhaps most of all, Alain Robbe-Grillet, now universally recognised as one of the most original and arresting minds in literature, and the central figure in the Parisian new school. His brilliant portrayal of objective reality as seen through the subjective mind in such novels as* **Jealosy, The Voyeur** *and* **The Erasers** *is also evidenced in his remarkable film,* **Last Year at Marienbad,** *of which we have published the text. Among other writers is Robert Pinget, a parallel figure*

calder authors

to Beckett, whose reputation will grow in the future. We know of no-one writing today who is quite so capable of conveying loneliness, despairing hope and futility as this admirable and poetic author. Both his **Three Plays** *and his novel* **No Answer** *have so far been published. Other French novelists whom we shall have the honour of presenting in translation include Louis René des Fortês, Claude Mauriac, Fernando Arrabal and René de Obaldia. We also publish one of the most charming of the lighter novelists, Monique Lange, whose* **The Plane Trees** *was very successful last year.*

Among other authors in translation are Simon Vestdijk, whose fine Dutch novel **Rum Island** *is just now ready to appear, and the short stories of a distinguished Italian Dinu Buzzati, a major contemporary figure, on his way to best-sellerdom.*

We have also published **The Blind Owl** of Sadegh Hedayat, the most remarkable work of Persian literature to appear since Omar Khayám. Soon we shall be introducing new writers from Germany and Spain, so that our catalogue will continue to grow with some of the very best new writers from other countries. Among our English language novels, we are especially proud of the Irish writer Aidan Higgins, whose short stories **Felo de Se** were acclaimed in 1960 as the most interesting work of a new writer to appear in a long time. His novel **Langrishe, Go Down** will be published this winter. Khushwant Singh is the outstanding Sikh writer of today and one of the principal talents from India. His novel **I Shall Not Hear the Nightingale** was a success with both critics and public and we anxiously await his next book. We also have some American novelists, notably Lars Lawrence, author of a series of novels set in New Mexico, entitled **The Seed.** Four parts have so far appeared and there are two still to come. Other American authors are Albert Maltz, Dola de Jong, James McGovern, Alvah Bessie and Paul Ableman.

We also publish some distinguished contemporary dramatists, most notably Eugene Ionesco, whose collected plays are available in four volumes in both hardcover and paperback editions; also Robert Pinget, whose **Three Plays** are just out, and Arthur Adamov, of whose work two volumes are in print here, **Paolo Paoli** and **Ping Pong.** Arrabal, a new French "beat" dramatist, will have four plays published by us soon. He brings a vein of savagery into plays of a Beckett-like formalism that has no parallel in the British drama today. The Calder authors at the festival are of course all novelists, as

at the festival

the International Writers' Conference is devoted this year to the novel, but they make a strong team: Alain Robbe-Grillet, Nathalie Sarraute, Khushwant Singh, Marguerite Duras, Louis René des Forêts and Alexander Trocchi (whose novel **Cain's Book** will appear this autumn). They are all novelists, who in their own way look to the future, and some of them have radically altered the shape of the novel for our time. If you are in any way interested in contemporary literature, we suggest that we should have your name on our mailing list, and that you simply send us a postcard with your name and address, saying "Please put me on your mailing list". Send it to JOHN CALDER (PUBLISHERS) LTD, 17 Sackville Street, London W.1 and we shall keep you informed.

angus wilson (a) If by 'literary' is meant book form I do not see any other more popular form at present. If other media are meant it is clear that as a popular form the novel lost some time ago in turn to the cinema and the television. As a serious art form the novel is founded in a protestant individualism which later changed to humanism. Powerful tho' the forces opposed to the individual as the centre of a metaphysic are today, I think it would be pessimistic to suppose that they are inevitably going to triumph (quite to the contrary) and the novel will therefore probably maintain its position if not regain some of its nineteenth-century force as an expression of a resurgent individualism.

(b) I don't believe in 'progress' in the arts—

(c) on the other hand I think that a serious novelist (as opposed to a competent, middlebrow one) will always want to do something new. Whether these attempts to do something new will be similar from one serious novelist to another I cannot say. I am against attempts to proselytise for one direction or another —either as C. P. Snow and his followers do for neo-traditionalism or as Robbe-Grillet and his followers for the anti-roman. I am inclined with other English novelists to suppose that the linguistic experiments of V. Woolf and Joyce, glorious tho' they were, have done all they can in English— perhaps the French will reach a similar point of discovery in a few years. I prefer to think that experiment will be with the fantastic and symbolic overtones of more traditional writers— Dickens, Balzac, etc. But I don't care to dogmatise on this. The novel lives only to express the individual and therefore everyman his own development. As to audience I suppose that the *popular* novel is a dying form superseded by the tele, etc. But with increased education, and especially the increased imagination that eventually follows education, the serious novel will have a wider audience, undeterred by any linguistic difficulties, indeed stimulated by them. At the moment we are at a stage of general education in W. Europe where the factual, and especially the pseudo-science of sociology appeals more than the deeper forces of imagination—hence the popularity of documentary or that bastard form documentary fiction over the novel proper. But I don't think it will last.

nathalie sarraute (a) I certainly do not believe that the novel is in danger. On the contrary, I believe that the development of the cinema and of television will oblige it to abandon fields into which it had no business to stray, and to become a truer form of art, purer and more independent.

(b) Like all forms of art, the novel will continue—for this is the very condition of its existence—to develop, to undergo a continual renewal of its substance and its form. But how is it possible to foresee the novel of the future? Who would have predicted that the works of Joyce or Proust would burst upon the world of literature they were to overturn?

(c) The development of new techniques will have the effect of sorting readers into their different categories. The novel will lose those who were seeking from it those things that no art can give; it will keep those willing to provide the effort and the co-operation that every living art must ask of its devotees.

kingsley amis (a) No I don't feel that the novel is in danger, certainly not from any competitors inside the field of lecture, though of course I don't know what effect future social change might have on this. But it would have to be a pretty major change.

(b) I tend to feel that all those concerned with 'the future of the novel', as with the future of most other things, rather beside the point. If we knew where we were going, we'd be there already. Still, as a private tip, I would expect to see some sort of blending of the serious novel with more popular forms, such as science fiction. But, like everybody else, I am probably just confusing what I think likely with what I think desirable or interesting.

(c) I don't know about new formal techniques. I thought we'd got over all that.

philip toynbee

I don't feel that the novel is dying, but I do believe that it will, and ought to, divide itself up into at least two quite separate forms. The sociological novel will always be of interest as one way of dealing with contemporary society. I don't think it has much future as an art form. The personal or poetical novel is really something altogether different. I think it will become more personal, rather than less, and therefore less intelligible to ordinary people. On the other hand one form or other of personal novel will be intelligible to a fairly large audience—enough, in any case, to keep this form going. And I need hardly say that this is the kind of novel which interests me and in whose ever-deepening future I am interested.

harold nicolson

In every decade during the last two centuries literary critics have said that the novel was no longer a channel of communication and had outlasted its appeal. In every case they have been proved wrong, and it has been shown that the novel is so popular a form of communication that although it may alter its methods it will never lose its appeal.

I imagine that the romantic novel is as dead as the novel of high life, but I suppose that there are infinite variations one can play on the novel of working-class life. I should imagine that the future appeal of the novel will be to a less intellectual audience and that therefore the style will become simpler rather than more complicated. But all prophecies regarding the future of any branch of literature are hopeless.

julian mitchell

(a) No. 'Is-the-novel-dead?' seems to me a mere game for literary journalists.

(b) Certainly it will continue to develop, and in all directions, I hope. The practice of individual novelists will determine the talking-points of those journalists not committed to the assumption that the novel is dead. The general direction of development will remain obscure (for those taking a longer view) for at least twenty years—and this will always be true.

(c) Not knowing what techniques you have in mind, or whether you refer to techniques as yet undiscovered, I can only say that

I doubt very much whether buying (and borrowing) habits are affected, or will be affected, by them, except, possibly, for hard-cover novels in the shortest of runs.

I hope this may be helpful, if not actually suggestive: I'm afraid I'm not very interested in present trends as such.

neil gunn (a) The novel as the dominant literary form will pass, like the epic and the ballad, when a more comprehensive way is found of telling the human story; at present there is no sign of this happening.

(b) The novel will continue to develop as the human story continues to discover its fate.

(c) The appearance of new formal styles and techniques, of the plotless plot and the story that is no-story, indicates both how alive as a form the novel is to the dangers of fixation and its search for the perfect form.

It is only by perfecting his technique that an artist attains freedom from it.

john braine I find your questions very difficult to answer, not because they aren't sensible questions, but because literature is something about which no-one can confidently make any firm predictions at all. One can only make predictions about social and economic trends, which may or may not affect the novel. However, I would say that

(a) there are no signs that the novel is losing its place as the dominant literary form. It may be true that less novels are being read; but the reason for this is not that the form is losing favour but that many of its practitioners are. If people are reading more non-fiction than fiction the reason is not a dislike of fiction as such but a dislike of the sort of fiction they are presented with.

(b) The novel must, like any other art form, continue to develop. If a writer fails to develop intellectually, to increase his understanding of the world around him, then he becomes sterile and does not even develop technically. So it is with the novel. I cannot tell you the direction of the novel's development but even as I write the words a hundred young novelists may be contributing to that development. I think myself that in England particularly the novel has a very long way to go. Its range is not wide enough, either in terms of background or in terms of emotional intensity. And English prose seems for the moment to have come to a dead end.

(c) If the new formal and stylistic techniques are used by novelists then they can only result in an increase of audience for the novelists. If, however, these techniques are adopted by people who are not really novelists at all, then the result will indeed be a loss of audience for these particular writers. But that, when I come to think of it, is nonsense. For you cannot be said to lose an audience which you never had.

muriel spark　　I am sorry to be unable to help you with the questions you ask. They look very interesting indeed, but I could not generalise on the subject at all, being too particularly involved with it, and not well-enough read in the modern novel. The only objective comment I can make is that the novel seems to be regarded more and more as a sort of basic story-capsule: if a novel intrigues the public imagination in book form, it becomes a play or film, and there is a radio and television version, and I see no reason why not opera and ballet versions. This may be good or bad according as the versions are good or bad. Some writers prefer to do their own adaptations to other forms. I prefer to leave mine to others, as it is a bore to go over the same thing again. It is easier to write something new.

'Needless to say that I am supremely indifferent to the "problems of a writer and the future of the novel" that are to be discussed at the conference.'
Quoted from a letter to *The Times*.
from **Vladimir Nabokov** dated 26 May 62

part two: programme

and biographical notes on the principal delegates to the conference

biographical notes pages 66-68 & 77-80

programme pages 69-73

list of delegates page 74

tribute to william faulkner page 75

durrell

miller

moravia

biographical notes

Lawrence Durrell *was born in India in 1912, and was educated at St. Edmund's School, Canterbury. He has lived in many countries and served the British Foreign Office in Athens, Cairo, Rhodes, Alexandria, and Belgrade. His last official post was Director of Public Relations, Government of Cyprus. He now lives in France. Durrell made his reputation first as a poet—his* **Collected Poems** *appeared in 1960—but has been most widely discussed as the author of 'The Alexandria Quartet': the novels* **Justine** *(1957),* **Balthazar** *(1958),* **Mountolive** *(1958), and* **Clea** *(1960).* **Bitter Lemons** *(1957) described his experiences in Cyprus.*

Henry Miller *was born in New York in 1891; after ten years of expatriate life in Europe (1930-40) he has lived in California since 1942. His first published work was* **Tropic of Cancer** *(1934). Later books include* **Black Spring** *(1936),* **The Cosmological Eye** *(1939),* **Tropic of Capricorn** *(1939),* **The Colossus of Maroussi** *(1941),* **The Air-Conditioned Nightmare** *(1945), and* **Big Sur and the Oranges of Hieronymus Bosch** *(1958).*

Alberto Moravia *was born in Rome in 1907. He worked for a time as a foreign correspondent in several European capitals. His first novel,* **The Time of Indifference,** *was published in 1929. Later novels have included* **The Fancy Dress Party** *(1941),* **Agostino** *(1944),* **The Woman of Rome** *(1947),* **Disobedience** *(1948),* **Conjugal Love** *(1949), and* **The Conformist** *(1951). He has also published several collections of short stories.*

Hugh MacDiarmid *was born in Langholm, in the south of Scotland, in 1892. He was the founding father in the nineteen twenties of the Scottish literary renaissance and remains today the dominant figure on the Scottish literary scene. His volumes of poems include* **Sangschaw** *(1925),* **Penny Wheep** *(1926),* **A Drunk Man Looks at the Thistle** *(1926),* **To Circumjack Cencrastus** *(1930),* **First Hymn to Lenin** *(1931),* **Second Hymn to Lenin** *(1932), and* **In Memoriam James Joyce** *(1955). His* **Collected Poems** *appears this year in Britain and America.*

Alain Robbe-Grillet *was born in Brest thirty-nine years ago. He took a degree at the Institut National Agronome, and has worked as an agricultural engineer in French Guinea, Morocco, Martinique and Guadaloupe. He is regarded as the pioneer and chief exponent of the 'nouveau roman'. His novels include* **Les Gommes, Le Voyeur, Jalousie, L'Année dernière à Marienbad,** *and* **Instantanés.**

Earl Russell, *pre-eminent among contemporary philosophers, has always been deeply concerned with the moral and political implications of art and life.*

Khushwant Singh *was born in what is now West Pakistan in 1915, and was educated at the Universities of Delhi, Punjab, and London. At different times he has practised as a lawyer, lectured on Law, served in the Indian Government, and worked for All India Radio and UNESCO. His novels include* **The Mark of Vishnu** *(1949),* **What's in a name?** *(1954),* **Train to Pakistan** *(1955), and* **I shall not hear the nightingale** *(1959).*

continued on page 77

earl russell photo pamela chandler

khushwant singh

robbe-grillet photo peter keen

programme   aug **20**

day one :
contrasts of
approach

Chairman: MALCOLM MUGGERIDGE

In this first discussion novelists will be asked to explain how they approach their work and why they try to write in a certain way. Some novelists are principally interested in the 'content' of their novels, in the ideas, the plot and the characters that they create, and regard 'style' as less important. Others see style as determining the nature of the content itself. The audience will hear the views of different authors on this and related problems.

The names of principal speakers on this day are separately announced.

Questions from the floor will be accepted towards the end of the discussion. Written questions will be taken to the chairman by the ushers.

bookstalls will be open in the foyer and basement of the McEwan Hall during the Conference

21 aug

programme

day two:

scottish writing today

What is the strength of Scottish writing today and how is it related to the Scottish literary tradition? Should Scottish writers deal principally with Scottish themes, and if they do, what market do they have outside Scotland? Has there been a Scottish Renaissance in recent years, and how successful have been the attempts to use Lallans as a literary language? These and other questions will be discussed.

Chairman: DAVID DAICHES

Speakers will include ROBIN JENKINS, WALTER KEIR, FIONN MACCOLLA, HUGH MACDIARMID, EDWIN MORGAN, NEIL PATERSON, ALEXANDER REID, ALEXANDER TROCCHI, DOUGLAS YOUNG.

Questions from the floor will be accepted towards the end of the discussion. Written questions will be taken to the chairman by the ushers.

bookstalls will be open in the foyer and basement of the McEwan Hall during the Conference

programme   aug 22

---

day three:
commitment

Chairman: STEPHEN SPENDER

Should the writer use his work as a platform for his political beliefs or his views on religion or other matters? Many believe that the novelist has a social duty to expose the evils of his time and to convert the reader to his opinions. Others believe that the novelist must be above such problems if he is to create a work of art, although he may be committed outside his work. The problem of commitment divides writers sharply and is one of the principal points of conflict in contemporary literature. A variety of views on both sides will be heard.

The names of principal speakers on this day are separately announced.

Questions from the floor will be accepted towards the end of the discussion. Written questions will be taken to the chairman by the ushers.

---

bookstalls will be open in the foyer and basement of the McEwan Hall during the Conference

23 aug

programme

---

day four :
censorship

Opinions on what may or may not be published differ widely. In Great Britain the censorship laws have recently been revised and previously banned books such as 'Lady Chatterley's Lover' can now be published. In America there has been an even greater relaxation of censorship and the same applies to many other countries, but there are still others where the trend is towards more censorship. Moral and political censorship will be discussed and writers will say how much censorship they think is desirable and where existing restrictions should be removed.

Chairman: MARY MCCARTHY

Speakers will include JAMES BALDWIN, WILLIAM BURROUGHS, ROBERT JUNGK, HUGH MACDIARMID, NORMAN MAILER, HENRY MILLER, ROBERTO FERNANDEZ-RETAMAR, ANGUS WILSON and others.

Questions from the floor will be accepted towards the end of the discussion. Written questions will be taken to the chairman by the ushers.

---

bookstalls will be open in the foyer and basement of the McEwan Hall during the Conference

programme   aug **24**

day five :
the novel and
the future

Chairman: To be announced

Speakers will include MICHEL BUTOR, ILYA EHREN-BURG, WILLIAM GOLDING, RAYNER HEPPENSTALL, ALDOUS HUXLEY, ROBERT JUNGK, COLIN MACINNES, ALBERTO MORAVIA, ALAIN ROBBE-GRILLET and others.

Many new trends in the novel have appeared in recent years and many types of 'avant-garde' novel have established themselves in critical and intellectual circles. Has the traditional novel really written itself out and will the public accept the new trends? Where are these trends leading us and why do so many contemporary novelists appear to create difficulties for their own sake? Will the novel perhaps disappear altogether and be replaced by some other literary form? These questions probe not only into the contemporary novel, but into all aspects of contemporary life and may point towards a solution to many of the problems of our time.

Questions from the floor will be accepted towards the end of the discussion. Written questions will be taken to the chairman by the ushers.

bookstalls will be open in the foyer and basement of the McEwan Hall during the Conference

list of delegates

Ivo Andric (YUGOSLAVIA)
George Andrzejewski (POLAND)
James Baldwin (U.S.A.)
Miodrag Bulatovic (YUGOSLAVIA)
William Burroughs (U.S.A.)
Michel Butor (FRANCE)
Truman Capote (U.S.A.)
David Daiches (SCOTLAND)
Jennifer Dawson (ENGLAND)
Tibor Déry (HUNGARY)
Louis René Des Forêts (FRANCE)
Heimeto von Doderer (AUSTRIA)
Marguerite Duras (FRANCE)
Lawrence Durrell (ENGLAND)
Ilya Ehrenburg (U.S.S.R.)
Erich Fried (AUSTRIA)
William Golding (ENGLAND)
L. P. Hartley (ENGLAND)
Rayner Heppenstall (ENGLAND)
Aldous Huxley (ENGLAND)
Robin Jenkins (SCOTLAND)
Robert Jungk (AUSTRIA)
Walter Keir (SCOTLAND)
Rosamund Lehmann (ENGLAND)
Mary McCarthy (U.S.A.)
Fionn MacColla (SCOTLAND)
Hugh MacDiarmid (SCOTLAND)
Colin MacInnes (ENGLAND)
Norman Mailer (U.S.A.)
Henry Miller (U.S.A.)
Naomi Mitchison (SCOTLAND)

Alberto Moravia (ITALY)
Edwin Morgan (SCOTLAND)
Neil Paterson (SCOTLAND)
Simon Raven (ENGLAND)
Alexander Reid (SCOTLAND)
Roberto Fernandez-Retamar (CUBA)
G. K. Zan Het Reve (HOLLAND)
Alain Robbe-Grillet (FRANCE)
Bertrand Russell (ENGLAND)
Nathalie Sarraute (FRANCE)
Petar Šegedin (YUGOSLAVIA)
Khushwant Singh (INDIA)
Izhar Smilansky (ISRAEL)
Muriel Spark (SCOTLAND)
Stephen Spender (ENGLAND)
Aleksandar V. Stefanovic (YUGOSLAVIA)
George Theotokas (GREECE)
Alexander Trocchi (SCOTLAND)
Nicka Tucci (U.S.A.)
Rex Warner (ENGLAND)
Angus Wilson (ENGLAND)
Douglas Young (SCOTLAND)

At the time of going to press, it is unfortunately not possible to include a final and definitive list of participants. Some novelists whose names are not included in this programme will probably attend at the last moment, while some of those announced may be unable to attend for a variety of reasons. The organisers much regret any inconvenience that may be caused to those who have come to hear any specific writer who is unable to be present.

the private genius of william faulkner

By W J WEATHERBY

The American novelist William Faulkner died on July 6th this year. We therefore felt it appropriate to include in our book a tribute to this great writer who incidentally was invited to attend this conference. We reprint the following article by kind permission of 'The Guardian', from their edition of Saturday 7th July 1962.

If William Faulkner had died before receiving the Nobel Prize, only a small group of fans would have mourned him. Now his sudden death in Oxford, Mississippi—or was it in Yoknapatawpha County?—calls for a tribute from the White House, even though Mr. Faulkner recently refused an invitation to dine there because, as he said, 'it's too far to go to eat with strangers'.

His long period of obscurity was due partly to the originality and complexity of his novels and partly to his refusal as a man to compromise in public relations. The Nobel Prize thrust him into the headlines in a way that perhaps could only happen in the United States, but Mr. Faulkner hardly altered his routine of farming and writing and giving the odd lecture to people he approved of. If Hemingway was the public genius in the American writing field, Faulkner was the private one: a man who perfectly mirrored the books he wrote.

He came from one of the aristocratic families of the Deep South—a family that had declined in a social sense like the Sartorises in his novels. He was born in New Albany, Mississippi, but soon afterwards his parents removed to Oxford where Faulkner attended high school, played with the idea of going to the university, but instead went off to the First World War in the Royal Canadian Air Force. When he returned to Oxford, he could not settle either as a man or as a writer. He tried odd jobs, he tried poetry, and then produced short stories in great quantities which he could not sell.

Sherwood Anderson—who with Mark Twain was one of the strongest influences on Faulkner's generation of American novelists—helped him to get his first novel, *Soldier's Pay*, published, but neither that nor the next two novels he wrote brought him any money. He had to borrow the money to get married and he was then in his early thirties. He decided not to try to write books that would sell but just to write the 'best I could', as he later described it.

The result was *The Sound and the Fury*, his own favourite among his books and often rated as the greatest. It is a complex study of the decline of a Southern family and highly experimental in technique, studying the same situation from several viewpoints and extending the range of stream of consciousness writing as used by Joyce. While stoking the furnace at night in a local power plant, he wrote *As I Lay Dying*, which again studied the decline of a family from multiple viewpoints.

He had realised by now, as he said recently, that 'I didn't need to write about interesting foreign places. There was more than enough in my own little postage stamp of earth to last me my lifetime.' And he settled down to write the great epic of the Deep South which he set in the mythical county of Yoknapatawpha.

For about ten years he wrote 'at the top of my talent' and produced *Light in August*, a vast novel about segregation (spiritual as well as social); *Absalom, Absalom*, more about the significance of the family; *Go Down, Moses*, which included his great short story of the wilderness which he used as a symbol of the past, *The Bear*; *The Unvanquished*, his tales of the Civil War which had marked Yoknapatawpha for eternity.... The titles perhaps are not too important for more than most novelists Faulkner must be read for the body of his work. The characters, the place, and the problems reappear in book after book, a reflection of the Faulkner saying that 'You must always know the past for there is no real Was, there is only Is'.

In his later life, when fame brought him reporters to jot down his most casual remarks, he was attacked for believing the South should solve its own racial problems. This was interpreted as meaning that Faulkner was really a go-slow Conservative. Any reader of the Yoknapatawpha saga will know his feelings about segregation. He was brought up as a boy with negroes and many of his stories reflected the deepest disgust with the behaviour of many of his fellow whites. His favourite character was Dilsey, the old negro grandmother in *The Sound and the Fury*, and probably his finest short story, *Pantaloon in Black*, described the heart-breaking grief of a young negro at the death of his wife which the whites completely misunderstand.

What Faulkner would not endorse was the claim of the North to be the civilised leader and the South as the blind bigot. He was a southerner who knew the reasons for the break-up of the old system and why the materialism he represented in his Snopes family had arisen. But the materialism was as much of the North as the South: the Yoknapatawpha characters had the guilt of slavery to work out for their salvation but in the end this was only a symbol of man's inhumanity, and this is where Faulkner's work rose to an international level. Other Deep South writers have written about the same situation and produced only local

fiction: Faulkner saw Mississippi in terms of the most uncompromising tragedy.

It was not the tragedy that made popularity elude him but his thick, often clotted style: in later life his sentences sometimes stretched for pages. He said recently: 'Part of the trouble is that I left school early and didn't do enough mathematics to get a properly disciplined mind, but I guess most of it is due to the fact that I tried to capture everything in every sentence. It was like trying to inscribe the whole of experience on the head of a pin. Something had to go and sometimes it was lucidity, sometimes it was the reader, and sometimes it was my point as a writer. I was never satisfied with anything I ever wrote. I always tried to say more than I had the talent to.'

After his great period up to the Second World War, he seemed to relax, wrote less, and what he did publish was more rhetorical and less tragic. As well as being a great tragedian, he is a humorist of the stature of Mark Twain, as his trilogy about the Snopes family shows, and more and more after fame came to him with the Nobel Prize, he used humour to reach his increasing audience. It was, as a friend remarked, 'as if Bill realised his best work was done and he could relax and enjoy himself as a writer'.

Although a reserved man who hated the phoniness of public life, he followed his family's tradition of fighting publicly any local threats to democracy as he saw it. In his great period he drank heavily, presumably to be able to live with so tragic a vision. He earned much of the money that enabled him to buy one of the old southern mansions in Oxford from Hollywood where he went occasionally to write scripts, including one or two for the late Humphrey Bogart. 'Writing for movies and television is a fine way to get a regular pay-check, but it has nothing to do with real writing,' he said recently.

These towering standards, both as writer and citizen, frightened many of his acquaintances, but they explain why he made such a mark—and so quietly—as both.

faulkner

biographical notes *continued from page 68*

Angus Wilson *was born in 1913 in the south of England. After leaving Oxford in 1937 he became a librarian in the British Museum. His first book, a collection of stories entitled* **The Wrong Set,** *appeared in 1949. In 1950 a second book of short stories,* **Such Darling Dodos,** *followed. His first novel,* **Hemlock and After,** *was published in 1952. Subsequent novels include* **Anglo-Saxon Attitudes** *(1956),* **The Middle Age of Mrs. Eliot** *(1958) and* **The Old Men at the Zoo** *(1961).*

William Golding *was educated at Marlborough Grammar School and Brasenose College, Oxford. At various times he has been schoolmaster, lecturer, actor, sailor (five years in the Royal Navy during the last world war), musician. His first novel,* **Lord of the Flies** *(1954), continues to be regarded as one of the most significant of contemporary English novels. Since 1954 Golding has published three other novels:* **The Inheritors** *(1955),* **Pincher Martin** *(1956), and* **Free Fall** *(1959).*

Aldous Huxley *was born in 1894, and educated at Eton and Balliol College, Oxford. In 1937 he moved to California where he still lives. His first novel,* **Crome Yellow,** *appeared in 1921. Later novels include* **Antic Hay** *(1923),* **Those Barren Leaves** *(1925),* **Point Counter Point** *(1928),* **Brave New World** *(1932),* **Eyeless in Gaza** *(1936),* **After Many a Summer** *(1939),* **Time Must Have a Stop** *(1945),* **The Genius and the Goddess** *(1955), and* **The Island** *(1962). He has also published several collections of essays and short stories.*

Rayner Heppenstall *is an English novelist, critic, and poet. His novels include* **The Blaze of Noon, The Greater Infortune** *and* **The Lesser Infortune.** **Léon Bloy** *and, his most recent work,* **The Fourfold Tradition** *(1961) are critical studies.*

Colin MacInnes *was born in London in 1914, and was brought up in Australia. He began writing after 1945—at first chiefly radio scripts for the B.B.C. His essays, mostly on the contemporary social scene, have appeared in such newspapers as* **The Times, The Guardian** *and* **The Observer** *as well as in magazines such as* **Encounter, Twentieth Century** *and* **The Spectator.** *His first book,* **To The Victor The Spoils,** *appeared in 1950. Later novels are* **June In Her Spring** *(1952),* **City of Spades** *(1957),* **Absolute Beginners** *(1959), and* **Mr. Love and Justice** *(1960).* **England, Half English,** *a selection of essays, was published in 1961.*

James Baldwin *was born in 1924. His first articles and stories began to appear in magazines such as* **Nation, The Reporter** *and* **Partisan Review,** *soon after the end of the last war. His first novel,* **Go Tell It On The Mountain,** *appeared in 1953. It was followed by* **Giovanni's Room** *in 1956.* **Notes of a Native Son** *(1955) is a collection of essays.*

Rosamond Lehmann *was educated privately and at Girton College, Cambridge. Her first novel,* **Dusty Answer,** *was published in 1927. Later novels are* **A Note in Music** *(1930),* **Invitation to the Waltz** *(1932),* **The Weather in the Streets** *(1936),* **The Ballad and the Source** *(1944),* **The Gypsy's Baby** *(1946), and* **The Echoing Grove** *(1953).*

L. P. Hartley *was born in England in 1895, and educated at Harrow and Balliol College, Oxford. His first novel,* Simonetta Perkins, *appeared in 1925. Later novels are* The Shrimp and the Anemone *(1944),* The Sixth Heaven *(1946),* Eustace and Hilda *(1947),* The Boat *(1950),* My Fellow Devils *(1951),* The Go-Between *(1953),* A Perfect Woman *(1955),* The Hireling *(1957), and* Facial Justice *(1960). He has also published several collections of short stories.*

Rex Warner *was born in England in 1905, and studied classics at Wadham College, Oxford. He became a schoolmaster and taught at schools both in England and abroad. His first book,* **The Wild Goose Chase,** *appeared in 1937. Later works include* **The Professor** *(1938),* **The Aerodrome** *(1941),* **Why Was I Killed?** *(1943),* **Men and Gods** *(1950),* **Greeks and Trojans** *(1951). He has also published translations of classical Greek drama and prose.*

golding photo coster

huxley

Stephen Spender *was born in England in 1909, and studied at University College, Oxford. Since the nineteen-thirties he has been known as a poet, critic, and editor. He is currently co-editor of* **Encounter.** *His* **Collected Poems** *appeared in 1955. Other works include an autobiography,* **World Within World** *(1951), and* **The Creative Element** *(1953).*

Naomi Mitchison *was born in 1897, and educated at the Dragon School, Oxford. Her many books include* **The Conquered** *(1923),* **Block Sparta** *(1928),* **Barbarian Stories** *(1929),* **The Delicate Fire** *(1933),* **We Have Been Warned** *(1935),* **The Blood of the Martyrs** *(1939),* **Re-Educating Scotland** *(1944),* **The Bull Calves** *(1947),* **The Swan's Road** *(1954),* **To The Chapel Perilous** *(1955),* **The Far Harbour** *(1957), and* **The Rib of the Green Umbrella** *(1960).*

Mary McCarthy *was born in Seattle and graduated from Vassar, class of 1935. She has been editor and theatre critic, and instructor in English at several American colleges. She is equally well known as essayist, novelist and critic. Her books include* **The Oasis, Cast a Cold Eye, The Groves of Academe, A Charmed Life, Venice Observed, Memories of a Catholic Girlhood,** *and* **On The Contrary.**

wilson

daiches

Norman Mailer *was born in New Jersey in 1923. He graduated from Harvard in 1943, and after service with the U.S. Army in the Pacific wrote* **The Naked and the Dead,** *published in 1948. Later novels are* **Barbary Shore** *(1951) and* **The Deer Park** *(1955). His most recent work is* **Advertisements for Myself** *(1959), a collection of essays and stories.*

Truman Capote *was born in New Orleans in 1925. His first novel,* **Other Voices, Other Rooms,** *appeared in 1948.* **The Grass Harp** *followed in 1951.* **Tree of Night** *(1949) and* **Breakfast at Tiffany's** *(1958) are collections of stories,* **Local Color** *(1950) a collection of travel sketches.* **The Muses Are Heard** *reports a visit to Russia.*

David Daiches *was born in Sunderland in 1912 and brought up and educated in Edinburgh. He attended Edinburgh University and Balliol College, Oxford, and has*

reid photo edin evening news

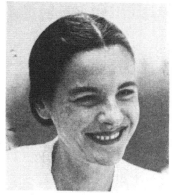

mccarthy

jenkins
photo martin, barcelona

mailer photo abc

duras

sarraut

since lectured on English Literature at several English and American universities. He is now Dean of the School of English and American Studies at the University of Sussex. He is the author of more than twenty books concerned with literature in England and America.

Alexander Reid was born in Edinburgh in 1914. He was educated at George Heriot's School, Edinburgh, and has worked in Scotland as a journalist and editor. He is the author of six plays, three of them written in Scots. 'The Lass wi' the Muckle Mou' and 'The World's Wonder' were published under the title **Two Scots Plays** in 1958. These plays have been widely produced and translated. Reid also writes plays and documentaries for radio.

Robin Jenkins was born near Glasgow and educated at Hamilton Academy and Glasgow University. He is now a school teacher in Dunoon. Many of his novels have been concerned with Scotland and the Scottish people—**The Thistle and The Grail, The Cone-Gatherers, Guests of War, The Missionaries** and **The Changeling**. His three most recent novels, however, **The Tiger of Gold, Dust on the Paw,** and **Some Kind of Grace**, reflect an interest in the Eastern scene generated by a stay in Afghanistan.

Walter Keir was born in 1920 and educated at Loretto, Aberdeen University and Merton College, Oxford. Now a Lecturer in English Literature at Aberdeen University, he is also a critic and broadcaster.

Edwin Morgan was born in Glasgow in 1920. He was educated at Glasgow High School and Glasgow University where he is now a Lecturer in English. He is a broadcaster and critic, and has published several collections of poems including **The Cape of Good Hope** (1955) and **Sovpoems** (1961).

Douglas Young was born in 1913. He is now Senior Lecturer in Greek at St. Andrews University. As a poet he is associated with Hugh MacDiarmid and the Scottish Renaissance movement. **Auntran Blads,** a collection of poems, appeared in 1943. **The Puddocks** (1957) and **The Burdies** (1959) are versions in Scots of Aristophanes' comedies.

Alexander Trocchi was born in Glasgow in 1925. He has lived and worked in Paris, Athens and elsewhere. For the past three years he has been living in the United States. **Young Adam** is his first novel to be published in England. **Cain's Book,** a novel of drug addiction, was published in America in 1960.

Muriel Spark was born in Edinburgh and was educated there at James Gillespie's High School for Girls. She spent several years in Central Africa, and worked for a time for the British Foreign Office. Her novels are **The Comforters** (1957), **Robinson** (1958), **Memento Mori** (1959), **The Bachelors** (1960), **The Ballad of Peckham Rye** (1960), and **The Prime of Miss Jean Brodie** (1961). **The Go-Away Bird** (1958) is a collection of stories, and **Voices at Play** (1961) of stories and radio plays.

Fionn MacColla was born in Montrose in 1906. For a number of years he taught in the Near East, and since 1940 he has been a headmaster in the Western Isles of Scotland. His first book, **The Albannach**, appeared in 1932. It was followed by **And the Cock Crew** in 1945, and **Scottish Noel** in 1958. **A Trial of Heretiks** will appear this year.

Nathalie Sarraute was born in Russia. She was educated in French schools and took degrees in English and Law at the Sorbonne. A leading exponent of the 'nouveau roman', her first book—**Tropismes**—was originally published in 1939. Later novels include **Portrait d'Un Inconnu** (1949), **Martereau** (1953), **L'Ere de Soupçon** (1958), and **Le Planetarium** (1959).

Michel Butor was born in France in 1926. He studied philosophy at the Sorbonne, and has since taught at several European universities. He is associated with the 'nouveau roman' movement, and his novels include **Passage de Milan** (1954), **L'Emploi du Temps** (1956), **La Modification** (1957), **Degrés** (1960), and **Histoire Extraordinaire** (1961).

Louis-René des Forêts was born in Paris in 1918. He studied Law and Political Science in the same city and has travelled widely in Europe. His first novel, **Les Mendiants**, appeared in 1943. **Le Bavard** followed in 1946, and **La Chambre Des Enfants** in 1960.

Marguerite Duras was born in Indo-China, and studied Mathematics at the Sorbonne. Associated with the 'nouveau roman' she is perhaps best known for her film scenarios—**Hiroshima Mon Amour**, **Une Aussi Longue Absence**, and **Moderato Cantabile**. Her novels include **La Vie Tranquille**, **Un Barrage Contre le Pacifique**, **Le Marin de Gibralta**, **Le Square**, **Dix Heures et Demie du Soir en Eté** and **L'Après-Midi de M. Andesmas**.

Jerzy Andrzejewski was born in Poland in 1909. His novels include **Harmony of the Heart** (1939), **Ashes and Diamonds** (1948), **Darkness Covers the Earth** (1957). **Night** (1945) and **The Golden Fox** (1955) are collections of stories.

Petar Šegedin was born in Croatia in 1909. He was educated in Split and Zagreb, and after completing his studies became a teacher in Zagreb. He began writing in 1937, and his novels, **God's Children** and **The Lonely Ones**, appeared in 1946 and 1947. **The Dead Sea** (1954) is a collection of stories.

Tibor Dery was born in Hungary in 1894. For political reasons he spent several years in exile, and during the period 1957–60 he was imprisoned. His novels include **Országuton, Szemtöl-Szembe, A Tengerparti Gyár, A Befejezetlen Mondat, Felelet I, II.** He is also the author of several collections of poems and short stories.

Ilya Ehrenburg was born in Russia in 1891. In the nineteen-twenties he was a correspondent for Soviet newspapers in Western Europe. His books include **The**

ehrenburg

jungk

Extraordinary Adventures of Julio Jurenito (1922), **Thirteen Trumpets** (1924), **Summer of 1925** (1926), **The Second Day** (1932), **What Man Needs** (1937), **Spanish Temper** (1938), **The Fall of Paris** (1942), **The Storm** (1949), **The Ninth Wave** (1952), and **The Thaw** (1954).

Ivo Andric was born in 1892, and educated at Zagreb, Vienna, Cracow, and Graz Universities. Before the last war he was a member of the Yugoslav diplomatic service. He was awarded the Nobel Prize for Literature in 1961. His books include **The Spinster, A Bosnian Story** (English trans. 1959), and **The Bridge on the Drina** (English trans. 1959).

George Theotokas was born in 1906, and educated at Athens, Paris and London Universities. His books include **Argo** (1936), **The Demon** (1938), **Leonis** (1940), **The Sacred Way** (1950), **An Essay on America** (1954), and **Problems of Our Time** (1956). He is also the author of several plays.

Heimeto von Doderer was born in Austria in 1896, and educated at the University of Vienna. His novels include **Ein Umweg** (1940), **Die erleuchteten Fenster oder die Menschwerdung des Amtsrates Julius Zihal** (1951), **Die Strudlhofstiege oder Melzer und die Tiefe der Jahre** (1951), and **Die Dämonen** (1956). He has also published several collections of poems.

Robert Jungk was born in Berlin in 1913, and was educated at the Gymnasium, Berlin University and the Sorbonne. Later he took a degree at Zurich University. His opposition to the Nazi régime forced him to leave Germany. He has had considerable experience in journalism and in film-making. His first book, **Tomorrow Is Already Here**, appeared soon after the end of the last war. It was followed by two books concerned with the dropping of the first atom bomb: **Brighter Than a Thousand Suns** (1956), and **Children of the Ashes** (1961).

part three: a survey of contemporary fiction

Since the eighteenth century the novel has been the literary form which has embodied the largest efforts of the creative imagination. It is to the novel that we turn to find the fullest definition, the truest image, of our society and ourselves. This is why the novel matters.

But dominance as a literary kind has also meant dominance in the printing presses. Most of us find it difficult enough to 'keep up' with the contemporary novel in one or, at most, two countries. So it is useful to hear from time to time what is going on elsewhere: who the young writers are, what kinds of novel they are writing, perhaps what trend is being followed or created. In the pages that follow, information of this kind is offered in relation to a wide variety of countries.* Of course the articles are not definitive, any more than the list of countries is. But they do together provide some account of 'the novel today'.

*The writers of the articles on India and Africa felt that the novel could not be discussed in isolation from the peculiar problems of the literary culture of these countries.

F

contents

africa and literature   83
GEORGE SHEPPERSON

the contemporary english novel   87
PRISCILLA JENKINS

the post-war french novel   91
LOUIS ALLEN

the post-war german novel   99
E F GEORGE

**contemporary indian writing
in english**   103
KHUSHWANT SINGH

the contemporary italian novel   107
KATHLEEN SPEIGHT

the post-war russian novel   111
RONALD HINGLEY

**american fiction since the
second world war**   117
MICHAEL MILLGATE

west indian novels   121
KARINA WILLIAMSON

africa and literature

by GEORGE SHEPPERSON

George Shepperson is Reader in Imperial and American history at the University of Edinburgh. With Thomas Price he is the author of 'Independent African; John Chilembwe and the origins, setting and significance of the Nyasaland native rising of 1915', published in 1958. Mr. Shepperson has also written widely on many aspects of American and African history and culture.

> . . . Africa is the unhistorical,
> Unremembering, unrhetorical,
> Undeveloped spirit involved
> In the conditions of nature . . .
>
> Edith Sitwell, *Gold Coast Customs* (1929).

When Edith Sitwell versified this passage—no doubt with the best will in the world—from Hegel's *Philosophy of History* on the eve of the Depression, she exemplified two attitudes towards the misnamed 'Dark Continent' from which African writers south of the Sahara—particularly black African writers—are now strenuously engaged in freeing themselves and, one hopes, their readers. The first is that, before the coming of the Europeans, Africa was one undifferentiated black mass, without history or hope. The other is the white man's habit of looking at Africa through Euro-American spectacles and *vice versa*: a mode of observation which makes it difficult, if not impossible, to regard Africa in its own right.

All new literatures begin with an inferiority complex. The new literatures of Africa have to struggle with this more than most. This battle began in the nineteenth century, particularly with Edward Blyden of Sierra Leone and Liberia in his *Christianity, Islam and the Negro Race* (1887). As European control of Africa and Western-style education developed, protests against these European-imposed concepts increased. J. E. Kwegyir Aggrey (1875–1927) is usually remembered for his image of racial co-operation: the analogy of the piano and the indispensability of playing on both the black and the white keys. Yet in his address to countless African audiences, his famous 'Parable of the Eagle', Aggrey sounded a more militant note: 'My people of Africa, we were created in the image of God, but men have made us think we are chickens, and we still think we are; but we are eagles. Stretch forth your wings and fly! Don't be content with the food of chickens!'

The most common European symbol of black Africa's inferiority has been its lack of the wheel or plough before the coming of the white man. This stuck in the throats of Negro intellectuals and was spewed forth on the eve of the 1939 War, when the white world, for all its inventiveness, was about to tear civilization apart, in the cry, 'Hurrah for those who never invented anything!' in Aimé Césaire's *Cahier d'un retour au pays natal*:

> Pitié pour nos vainquers omniscients et naïfs!
>
> Eia pour ceux qui n'ont jamais rien inventé
> pour ceux qui n'ont jamais rien exploré
> pour ceux qui n'ont jamais rien dompté
>
> Eia pour la joie
> Eia pour l'amour
> Eia pour la douleur aux pis de larmes réincarnés

Césaire's impassioned words touched off the nearest thing to a school which African writing has yet produced: *négritude*. This, so far as it is capable of definition, has been called 'a certain quality which is common to the thoughts and behaviour of Negroes; the new consciousness of the

Negro'. Maturing amongst Negro intellectuals from the French colonies in Paris, it produced in 1948 a monument to *négritude* in *Anthologie de la nouvelle poésie nègre et malgache*, to which Sartre contributed an influential foreword, 'Orphée Noir'. The editor was Léopold Sédar Senghor, now President of an independent Senegal.

The year before, the first number was produced—also in Paris and by another Senegalese, Alioun Diop—of *Présence africaine*, a journal which, through its exploration of the African past and present, has influenced intellectuals of Negro descent everywhere. In 1956 it organized in Paris the First International Congress of Negro Writers and Artists; and a Second Congress in Rome in 1959. They produced two important groups of resolutions that constitute a manifesto for the African literature that is to come.*

Already, however, there are signs of restiveness with *négritude*. Prominent amongst its critics is Ezekiel Mphahlele, a refugee from South Africa in Nigeria, who stresses the uniqueness of the artist, condemns racialist mystique and scorns the search for the pre-European past of Africa. Indeed, he goes so far as to compare this to the tendency of Afrikaans culture in his own country. 'Our music', he says, meaning, presumably, the eclectic compositions best known outside South Africa by Todd Matshikiza's *King Kong*, 'will always be more vital . . . than *boere-musick* (Afrikaans music) which is a monument to the dead past, full of false posturing.'†

That such a criticism of *négritude* should have come from a black South African illustrates a comment which is often made: *négritude* came from the French territories where colonial policy had striven to produce a rootless *élite*, black Frenchmen, and not from British Africa where a policy of indirect rule had, to a considerable extent, preserved traditional institutions. The Paris-orientated French African intellectual, having been torn out of his past, was determined to recreate it; the British African, having more of it about him, was less concerned to discover it.

But this generalization can be over-emphasized. British West Africans participated in the 1956 and 1959 Conferences; there are movements for the study and revitalization of Akan and Yoruba poetry; Ibadan has produced a literary journal with a title, *Black Orpheus*, redolent of Sartre's introduction to the 1948 French anthology; and there is a keen and able group of historians, in which the names of K. O. Dike and S. O. Biobaku stand out as pioneers, devoted to the study of the African past.

Nevertheless, the literature which is now appearing in former British West Africa has a generally more pragmatic and less theoretical approach than that from the old French territories. If one compares the work, for example, of Camara Laye from Guinea and Amos Tutuola from Nigeria, the contrast is apparent. Superficially, in their preoccupation with traditional life and their search for symbolical overtones in it, they seem to have much in common. But Laye's *The Dark Child* (1953) and *The Radiance of the King* (1956)—to quote their English translations—have a polish and structure which is totally lacking in Tutuola's 'nativist' *Palm Wine Drinkard* (1952) or *My Life in the Bush of Ghosts* (1954). Indeed, it is significant that Tutuola, with his racy idiom, has his greatest support outside Africa—Dylan Thomas was one of his earliest admirers—whereas, in Nigeria, he is looked upon as a literary aberration.

The main stream of the new writing of former British West Africa is represented by a group of Nigerian novelists who are, in their way, as occupied with two cultures as their British counterparts. This is illustrated in the titles of the major works of Chinua Achebe: *Things Fall Apart* (1958) and *No Longer At Ease* (1960). It is equally apparent in

* To be found in translation with a sympathetic review of contemporary African cultural problems in Colin Legum, *Pan-Africanism* (London: Pall Mall Press, 1962. 27s. 6d.), pp. 212-220.

† *The African Image* (London: Faber, 1962. 21s.), p. 28. For all its shortcomings, this highly personal volume provides a useful introduction to recent African literature and reminds us in its examination of white South African writers, including such exiles as Doris Lessing, that other literatures than those by black writers are coming out of Africa. An unexplored subject in English, however, is the literature of Portuguese Africa, particularly of the *asimilado*.

Cyprian Ekwensi's *People of the City* (1954) and *Jagua Nana* (1961); or in Onuora Nzekwu's more traditional *Wand of Noble Wood* (1961).

But the writers who catch the reviewers' eyes, whether they are from British or French West Africa, have one thing in common: they use the language of the former colonial power.

This is not to say that there has been no interest in vernacular writing. In addition to Swahili and Hausa poetry in Arabic script before the coming of the European, there have been extensive experiments in the vernacular, especially in the British territories. These have included not only transcriptions of oral poetry and tradition—J. H. Kwabena Nketia's work on Akan poetry, for instance—but also the employment of vernaculars in versions of European literary modes: for example, Thomas Mofolo's novel in Sesuto, *Chaka* (1927; translated, 1931); Samuel Y. Ntara's Cewa narrative, *Headman's Enterprise* (translated, 1949); the Zulu poetry of B. W. Vilikazi; and the unique experiment in epic verse in Shona, *Soko Risina Musoro (The Tale without a Head*, translated, 1958) by Herbert Chitepo. Yet vernacular writing may be fighting a losing battle with English and French.

If African writing to-day is driven forward by predominantly local forces—not the least of which is the necessity to satisfy ever-increasing reading publics—it is still open to influence by external forces, particularly the example of other writers of African descent. West Indian influences have made a permanent mark on the emergence of a new African literature: Blyden was a West Indian; Césaire is from Martinique; and René Maran, whose novel, *Batoula* (1922) influenced much of the French African fiction of social protest, was of Guiana descent. Indeed, sometimes the West Indies spell can take an African writer away from his allegiance altogether, as seems to have happened with Peter Abrahams, the Cape Coloured novelist, who, from his *Song of the City* (1942) to his *Wreath for Udomo* (1956) dominated much of the English-speaking African literary world but has now settled in Jamaica. It remains to be seen whether the post-War burgeoning of British West Indian writing will add new traits to the already established Caribbean mark on African literature.

Similarly, the literature of the Negro American has influenced African writing, particularly by its exploration of the Negro past and by its models for a literature of social protest. Four names stand out. The first is W. E. B. Du Bois, whose *Souls of Black Folk* in 1903 anticipated the comment by a modern Negro writer that *négritude* is 'anti-racist racism'[*] by speaking of 'that vaster ideal that swims before the Negro people, the ideal of human brotherhood, gained through the unifying ideal of Race' and who, at the age of 93, went to Ghana to edit an encyclopædia of the Negro. The second is the Harlem poet, Langston Hughes, whose verse is quoted all over Africa, particularly in the literary flourishes of political speeches and manifestos. Thirdly, there is Richard Wright, whose novels of protest, such as *Black Boy* (1945), had been powerful influences on socially-conscious African writing, but who, when he spoke at the 1956 Conference of Negro Writers, appeared to many Africans in his audience to be the voice of America—if not 'The Voice of America'—rather than of a new Africa. Wright himself was a victim of that 'tragic élite' which was the subject of his address. And finally, there is James Baldwin, novelist and critic, who also attended the 1956 Conference and reported it, with something of Mphahlele's spirit, in his *Nobody Knows My Name* (1961). Baldwin's writing raises in an acute form the problem of values implicit not only in the American Negro's struggle for integration into United States' society but also for the African battle for independence in a world of competing materialisms.

It is this crisis of values which makes itself felt throughout African writing to-day. At the foot of the statue of President Nkrumah in Accra is written, 'Seek ye first the political Kingdom'. Do these words imply the absence of spirituality in the new Africa? Or is it possible that they stand for a new kind of spirituality, the sort that is indicated in the last section of Alejo Carpentier's novel of the revolution in Haiti, the first black republic, *The Kingdom of this*

[*] Quoted in Legum, *op. cit.*, p. 95.

World (1957): 'In the Kingdom of Heaven there is no grandeur to be won, inasmuch as all is established hierarchy, the unknown is revealed, existence is infinite, there is no possibility of sacrifice, all is rest and joy. For this reason . . . man finds his greatness . . . only in the Kingdom of this World'? Or does the final gloss remain with the Shona spokesman in *Soko Risina Musoro*: 'As blind men let us walk, let us walk and be humble in the darkness which is before us whither we go, the darkness which is behind whence we have come. God alone is the light'?

Whatever is the answer, it is such questioning which, as for all literature, supplies the materials for the African masterpieces to come. It may be that they will spring out of the vernaculars. It may also be that we must await an African Conrad who will seize not only on the subtleties of a foreign language as his instrument but will peer deep in the cultures of the former masters to show that, in essence, the heart of the darkness is also the heart of the light.

the contemporary english novel

by PRISCILLA JENKINS

Priscilla Jenkins is a member of the Department of English of the University of Edinburgh.

The only obvious 'trend' in English fiction at the moment is expressed in the work of writers such as John Braine, Alan Sillitoe, Kingsley Amis, John Wain, and William Cooper. These novelists all show a sociological understanding of contemporary English life and treat it with strict realism. This similarity of position is clear in spite of the great differences in temperament between them: Braine, for example, in *Room at the Top*, writes with great moral seriousness, Amis and Wain with humour which sometimes degenerates into farce, Cooper with irony. I think the best novel of this group is *Room at the Top*, the story of a man who sacrifices love and self-respect to material success and realises sharply what has happened to him. Sillitoe, in *Saturday Night and Sunday Morning*, shows a real understanding of the character of his factory-worker hero, but his compassion and sense of drama are given far more scope in the short stories, particularly *The Loneliness of the Long-Distance Runner*. Apart from these, I do not usually find novels of this type very satisfying. They often seem to present life in narrowly behaviouristic terms. With the exceptions I have indicated, these novelists are realistic only in the narrowest sense. Great novels give you a sense of why people act as they do, what emotional states feel like, how relationships evolve. Amis most clearly shows his lack of interest in such questions in *Lucky Jim*: when Christine says that she does not know what love means, Jim replies, 'It's a word you must often have come across in conversation and literature. Are you going to tell me it sends you flying to the dictionary each time? . . . If you can tell me whether you like greengages or not, you can tell me whether you're in love with Bertrand or not.' This superficiality accounts for the limitations of his latest novel *Take a Girl Like You*. One recognises the accuracy of the situation, the thoughts and the actions of the characters. But as the author never explores the girl's desire to keep her virginity one is uncertain whether he intends the loss of it to seem pointless or, as is briefly hinted in her thoughts after the event, an acceptance of the compromises of grown-up life. The failure of this group of novelists to investigate questions of value and motive is also seen sharply in Malcolm Bradbury's *Eating People is Wrong*. The book begins most successfully as a comic portrait of modern university society (and is more convincing in this respect than *Lucky Jim*), but it falls apart when the author attempts to show the dilemma of the liberal intellectual in the modern world as serious and painful.

C. P. Snow has much in common with these novelists although unlike them he writes of the Establishment, of Cambridge, the upper reaches of the Civil Service, top scientists. *Strangers and Brothers*, a sequence of written and projected novels, deals with important public events over the last thirty years or so and with the personal life of the narrator Lewis Eliot and some of his friends. The scheme is ambitious only in scope. In itself it presents an artificiality which limits its attempted realism: the novels are not divided chronologically but according to subject so that their duration often overlaps. As Bernard Bergonzi pointed out in *Twentieth Century*, it is incredible that a character involved in so many lives and events as Lewis Eliot could separate them into mental compartments in this way. We can have no sense of him as an integrated person. Elsewhere Snow is conspicuously unable to create characters. Roy Calvert, the subject of *The Light and the Dark*, communicates to the reader none of the emotions which he is said to evoke in the narrator. Although scattered through the books are psychological observations of surprising wisdom these have an epigrammatic force and rarely seem related to the cardboard creatures they explain. In general Snow fails to convince, but there are exceptions, for example, Eliot's relationship with his first wife in *Homecomings*, and he can involve us in his own probably discreditable interest in struggles for power.

More fully imaginative writers are too individual to fit into such categories. It seems better to speak of them one by one, giving more space to novelists who have emerged during the last ten years and who may go on to produce their most important work in the future.

Some novelists who were already established before the war have continued to develop since.* Evelyn Waugh has become a more superficially serious novelist with *Brideshead Revisited*, *The Ordeal of Gilbert Pinfold* and *Men at Arms*, a trilogy about the last war, though none of these seem to me to be as good as his early satires. Joyce Cary's post-war trilogy (*Prisoner of Grace*, *Except the Lord* and *Not Honour More*) presents, like his other work, vividly imagined characters and a deep and convincing communication of the Puritan conscience. L. P. Hartley's best work is the *Eustace and Hilda* trilogy, particularly the first volume about Eustace's childhood, and *The Go-Between*, the story of a boy's loss of innocence set in the summer of 1900. Rather unexpectedly Hartley has recently written a fantasy about the future, *Facial Justice*. His conception of a state dominated by guilt and fear of individual excellence after the third world war is psychologically powerful but the characters are much less interesting than the picture of their society. Anthony Powell's novel sequence *The Music of Time* shares the satiric brilliance of his early books but is far more ambitious in its concern

* I shall not discuss other important novelists, such as Ivy Compton-Burnett, who are still writing in much the same style.

with the unexpected developments in human personality and the fortuitous character of meetings and re-meetings. Graham Greene has written two of his most important novels since the war, *The Heart of the Matter* and *The End of the Affair*. Scobie's dilemma in *The Heart of the Matter* seems central to Greene's thought and the setting, typical of most of his novels in its squalor and corruption, is explained as the least misleading image of the human situation. I find *The End of the Affair* Greene's most powerful novel in spite of the chain of miracles at the end of the book. In one sense it can hardly be said to operate as a novel at all in that Sarah's sanctification is presented as psychologically inexplicable. Greene's latest novel, *A Burnt-Out Case*, reads almost like an imitation of himself: it seems to me to have none of the intensity that made the earlier novels, however questionable their presentation of moral problems, so deeply moving.

William Golding, Angus Wilson and Iris Murdoch seem to me to be the most important new novelists. Golding's four novels are explorations of man's inherent evil. The first three have a kind of mythic quality: each shows humanity in some isolated setting in which its nature is most clearly seen. *The Lord of the Flies* is about a group of boys marooned on an island. In one sense they gradually shed the habits of the civilisation they have left and degenerate into savages; in another sense they move through all the stages of civilisation, from vegetarianism to the expression of their sadistic instincts in hunting, from a desire for order to a police state with its dictator and torturer. In fact the world they have left is no better, for all its adult façade of civilisation. The boys' plight on the island is due to war; the officer who rescues them at the end comes from a ship armed with sub-machine-guns. *The Inheritors* is an attempt to show a turning point in prehistory. While the humanist may see the evolution of man as a progressive improvement the question that occurs to the Christian is, When did man become capable of sin? Golding's new men are full of initiative but their instincts are hostile and predatory. Not all their achievements can atone for 'the darkness of man's heart'.

88

In *Pincher Martin* Golding examines the same question from a different position. Instead of showing the processes of evil in a society he concentrates retrospectively on one life. The book opens with a description of a man drowning in the Atlantic. Washed on to a rock he struggles for some days to remain alive and we see delirious flashbacks of his former life. At the end of the book it is disclosed that Martin died instantly in the water and the story assumes a more sinister aspect: Martin's clinging to life reveals his unwillingness to accept that he is dead, his rapacious existence on the rock is a hell or purgatory of his own making. *Free Fall*, Golding's latest novel, is less successful. In it he attempts to discover the moment at which his hero chose to fall. It is uncertain whether Golding can write, as here, about ordinary life, whether he does not need the special isolation of an island, a rock or a primitive community to work out his doctrine of depravity. This view would seem to be supported by the flashbacks to Pincher Martin's earlier life which have none of the vividness and emotional force of his nightmare rock. In general one may question Golding's absorption in evil. One may feel that he seriously underestimates the impulses to order and to love, that in doing so he gives a distorted account of human nature.

In his earlier stories and novels Angus Wilson showed an awareness of evil as powerful as Golding's if not as profound. His short stories present a very varied exposure of human wickedness, folly and hypocrisy. Some of them are sadistic in the extreme but they are also highly comic, although Wilson is not always able to resist a tendency to employ bludgeon as well as rapier ('She was not quite sure that her angora jumper was exactly right, but at any rate her pearls—a twenty-first birthday present from Daddy—were really good.') In Wilson's first two novels *Hemlock and After* and *Anglo-Saxon Attitudes* we are in a world of fierce contrast between good and bad, an uneven conflict since the good are weak and ineffectual whereas the bad are forceful and compelling. Indeed Wilson's evil characters are often monsters, grotesque Dickensian caricatures, frozen in one attitude of malice. Although both these novels have a huge

dramatis personae the central character is almost the only human being. In *Hemlock and After* Bernard Sands, a liberal humanist, is unable to affect large areas of evil and unreason around him. The climax of the book is when he feels a sadistic impulse and realises that he too is evil. After his death we are made to feel that he has had little influence on the people who knew him. *Anglo-Saxon Attitudes* has a very similar structure but the impression given by the book is surprisingly one of optimism. In his personal relationships the historian Gerald Middleton is as much a failure as Bernard Sands but he is somehow saved, in his own eyes and the reader's, by his final exposure of an archaeological fake. Wilson has documented his account of this excavation with exhilarating thoroughness and succeeds in convincing us that the integrity of his hero depends on one scholarly detail. *The Middle Age of Mrs. Eliot* is written in a completely new manner. Compared with the first two it seems very subdued. It is more conventional and detailed in its treatment of psychological states. Situations are fully explained rather than being hinted in a swift innuendo or a bitchy remark. The author's attitudes to his characters is one of tolerance, not condemnation. This all contributes to a very impressive portrait of the widowed heroine and, in David, to a kind of celebration of the virtues of passivity, even though the book is not as obviously entertaining as its predecessors.

Iris Murdoch's novels can be seen as an investigation of the conditions of human action. In *Under the Net* Jake is moved by the principle of attraction, spellbound by Hugo and Anna, until he can see them as human beings and accept his own life. In *The Flight from the Enchanter* the principle is repulsion. Although it is as witty and inventive as *Under the Net* the effect is less successful: Misha, the enchanter of the title, from whom the other characters are in flight, should be as compelling as Hugo. In fact it is difficult to believe in his sinister power. The book is violently centrifugal without really having a centre and tends to fly apart into dazzling but unrelated fragments. *The Sandcastle*, *A Severed Head*, and *An Unofficial Rose* are studies in freedom: *The*

Sandcastle demonstrates that the hero, a creature of habit, is not really free to leave his wife; the action of *A Severed Head* shows a persistent rejection of restraints; *An Unofficial Rose* presents both possibilities in the husband who goes and the wife who waits, as well as other shades of possibility in at least a dozen more examples of loving. *The Bell* is less easily summed up but the problems it raises are set out in the two sermons which take the bell as their symbol. The events in the novel seem to support Michael's plea for acting in the best way one *can* with a knowledge of one's own character, rather than James's advocacy of an obedient and unthinking innocence. It is perhaps misleading to sum up these novels so abstractly: at their best they give a very strong impression of the actuality of their characters and settings. Seen in its context the title of *Under the Net* is a condemnation of theorising which can only lead away from actuality. There is also in all these novels a strong sense of the power of un-reason. Sometimes this is intrusive: it is unnecessary to in-troduce the gipsy and the wax effigy into *The Sandcastle* as if the love affair were destroyed by external malignity. Some-times it is badly handled. In *A Severed Head* three couples work out almost every possible permutation of partners with the effect of an elegant minuet. This form does not seem entirely appropriate to the dark irrational love which the hero discovers in himself for Honor Klein and the oriental imagery of severed heads and swords never quite fuses with this character. Furthermore the London-society and country-houses setting is sentimentally described. There is a deep disharmony between the lives of the characters and the discoveries that the hero makes about life, a disharmony that cannot be explained away as a contrast between the conventional and the real. Iris Murdoch seems to have two main talents, for psychological exposition and for comic or poetic fantasy. These elements are combined in different ways and with different degrees of success in all her novels. At her best, in *Under the Net* and *The Bell*, the combination is very impressive indeed.

Lawrence Durrell's *Alexandria Quartet* has been more admired on the continent than in England. In many ways it seems to belong to the French tradition, particularly in its debt to Proust. These four novels present an illustration in fiction of the principle of relativity. With his multiplicity of narrators Durrell points out that the same event or character can be quite different from different points of view. Leaving aside the question of how far such a theory fatally detracts from the responsibility of the author, one may object that the characters are too incredible to make this treatment of them particularly interesting. We have little apprehension of them as people. They talk either in weak epigrams ('Damn the word,' said Justine once. 'I would like to spell it backwards as you say the Elizabethans did God. Call it "evol" and make it part of "Evolution" or "revolt". Never use the word to me.') or in huge tragic utterances ('Diseases are not interested in those who want to die.' 'We use each other like axes to cut down those we really love.') The most memorable feature of the *Quartet* is the portrait of Alexandria, squalid, romantic and mysterious, described in blurred passages of fine writing.

Muriel Spark writes macabre comedies of which *Memento Mori* is probably the best. She usually avoids the subject of love by writing of groups of people such as con-firmed bachelors or the very old. In *The Prime of Miss Jean Brodie* the sexual life of the main character is commented on by her young pupils with distinctly comic effect.

In conclusion, one may say that the most interesting novelists today show a concern with fantasy (for example, novels about the future such as *Facial Justice* and Wilson's latest book, *The Old Men at the Zoo*), philosophy (Iris Murdoch, Durrell, Nigel Dennis in *Cards of Identity*), religion (Golding, Greene, Iris Murdoch in *The Bell*, Muriel Spark). One also notices a number of good minor novels dealing with mental illness (for example, Jennifer Dawson's *The Ha-ha*, John Rosenberg's *Mirror and Knife*, Thomas Hinde's *Mr. Nicholas*). Such subjects which can hardly be treated with great naturalism seem to preoccupy the most imaginative novelists at present.

the post-war french novel

by LOUIS ALLEN

Louis Allen is Senior Lecturer in French at Durham University.

June 22nd 1940 might well be chosen as the watershed of the modern French novel. It is a date which has nothing to do with syntactical or structural experiments, nothing to do with vocabulary or rhythm. It is simply the date on which the armistice was concluded with a victorious Germany. The defeat of France in 1940 not only seemed to confirm the tragic social and political sickness of a nation which could no longer defend itself; in the humiliation of that defeat and of the occupation which followed lay the seeds of most of France's present problems and of the literature which reflects them.

Not that all her recent literature *has* reflected them. But the novel, because of its very range and extension, is the genre most capable of holding a mirror to the times, and it is worth while looking at the growth of the French novel since the war from this particular point of view. In some ways it gives a surer dividing line of sensibility than the criterion of experiment, which is the most conspicuous 'export' feature of the recent French novel. An averagely well-informed English reader who would expect to be familiar with, say, Butor, Robbe-Grillet, Claude Simon, Nathalie Sarraute, or Marguerite Duras would find in them—and with good reason—his main interest in the novel considered as an exploration of its own possibilities, as an art which, like the poetry of Mallarmé, is a fundamental calling into question of its own nature through experiments in technique and vision. And even though he might find the claims tacitly made for their originality somewhat overdone, hearing echoes of Virginia Woolf in Nathalie Sarraute (whose *Tropismes*, incidentally, like Sartre's *La Nausée*, dates back as far as 1938), and of Apollinaire's poem *Zone* in Butor's use of the second person as the narrator pronoun, he would see that the shift of focus in the work of these novelists is certainly a considerable one. It involves the dissolution of the narrator, the dissolution of the narrative itself, and the banishment of the psychology of the person in favour of the Ponge-like notation of the intricacies of the autonomous object.

He is less likely to have come across, say, Jean-Louis Curtis, Hervé Bazin, or Jean Dutourd, largely because they are bound up with the times much more closely. The texture of their work is much more heavily laden with contemporary and local reference which does not easily cross the Channel. It is with this secondary field of the French novel that this article deals: with novelists who are still concerned with a thread of orthodox narrative, with the creation of character in the classical sense, with the depiction of a social milieu (whether it be infused with a particular metaphysic or not), with satire and realism—a surface realism, certainly, if we regard Robbe-Grillet's banishment of the human and a close penetration of the object as the only true realism.

For this type of novel the experience of war, of defeat, of occupation and resistance is crucial. It provides the narrative skeleton, for example, of Sartre's *Les Chemins de la liberté* (1945–1949). This work, which was planned as a tetralogy, has tailed away in a few instalments of *Les Temps modernes* and looks as if it will never be finished, presumably because the stage offers its author a more immediately rewarding fictive expression and pamphleteering absorbs the rest of his energies. And this is a pity, because with all its faults, its overdone imitations of the style of Dos Passos in the second volume (*Le Sursis*), Sartre's tremendous verve in creating situations and his penetrating analysis of certain

91

psychological moments could have made this one of the French novel's major achievements. As it stands, it is an enormous fresco of French life from just before Munich to the German invasion, seen from the point of view of three main characters each of whom is engaged on seeking freedom. Mathieu, a philosophy teacher, is occupied throughout the first volume, *L'Age de raison*, with the problem of how to preserve his freedom now that his mistress, Marcelle, is pregnant and he has to decide whether and how to procure an abortion for her. He finishes up as a soldier, in the third volume, taking his revenge on life for his failure to find freedom, by firing angrily and hopelessly from a church tower into the advancing Germans, the only liberty he has found being the inflicting of terror. Daniel, the homosexual, offers to marry Marcelle for much the same reason as he has thought of castrating himself, in order to deny his homosexuality, to alter the being he feels he is in the eyes of others (the notion of the individual consciousness becoming vulnerable, 'objectified' in the gaze of others, is central to Sartre's philosophy): an act of bad faith and revealed as such when Daniel is repelled by Marcelle's body on their honeymoon and leaves her. Mathieu and Daniel relate their own stories; the world of Brunet, the dedicated Communist, is narrated by Mathieu, from the outside, as of someone who has had the courage to fix himself in a permanent choice—the echo of a perennial unsolved debate for Sartre himself. But Brunet is disillusioned by the Nazi-Soviet pact and ends by resisting the Nazis in a prison camp. Sartre impresses by the sheer multiplicity of his talents, the ability to mingle acute philosophical and psychological speculation with political gossip and then suddenly switch to minutely detailed recreation of the physical sensation—nausea, orgasm, clamminess—in a variety of styles, colloquial dialogue and 'stream of consciousness' together with the simultaneist presentation of speech and thought of characters remote and unconnected with one another. Structurally speaking, the series is a tremendous *tour de force*.

Camus' *La Peste* (1947) at first sight seemed a very obvious allegory of the German occupation in the descent of the plague on the Algerian town of Oran, from the first menacing spectacle of rats' corpses multiplying in the streets to the final retreat of the disease and the survivors coming out of the beleaguered city into life again. But although the novel's immediate success was no doubt partly the result of this parallel with an experience his readers had recently lived through, Camus—unlike Sartre who is totally occupied with the detailed present—uses both the plague and the Occupation it evokes as a massive twin symbol of the presence of evil in the world of men, both the evil men cause and the evil caused in spite of men. Certain significant figures bear the burden of the plague: the journalist Rambert who is tempted by desire for his mistress, left behind in Paris, to leave the city and return to her, and finally refuses to do so because he is afraid of the shame of being happy alone; Father Paneloux, the figure of the Christian who tries to reconcile the suffering he sees with the God he knows and is broken in the attempt; Tarrou (in some ways almost a parody of the development of Camus himself), who faces what he regards as an absurd universe with a resigned lucidity which changes into revolt as he contemplates the repeated suffering of the innocent; and the unobtrusive narrator Rieux who knows he cannot change the evil in the world but, as a doctor, the symbolic alleviator of other men's evil, goes about his work of healing to shore up a tiny morsel of hopeless hope. Both Rieux and Tarrou exemplify in their separate ways Camus' human ideal of 'the saint without God'.

Camus' skill as a novelist had already been seen in the brief *L'Étranger* (1942) with its evocation of a meaningless world where actions are dictated by caprice and the indifference of material objects and events and not by any definite moral choice on the part of the individual, a world in which the actions of the 'hero' Meursault seem to be taking place at one remove from himself. When he commits a murder and is condemned to death for it he feels quite uninvolved, and it is only on the threshold of his death that life takes on a reality for him. But *La Peste* opens many more stops than Camus used in his first novel and combines the medical realism of the plague—treatments, death agonies, burials—with a series of dialogues and meditations on man's position in an absurd world in which all he has is the banal and despairing hope—Camus' own—that 'there are more things in man to admire than to despise'.

Camus' later fiction is ambiguous enough, like his later views on his native Algeria, to have given rise to many different interpretations. Both the sardonic bitterness of *La Chute* (1956) and the grim irony of some of the stories in *L'Exil et le royaume* (1957) seem to indicate a fundamental cleavage within himself, an inability to adopt an attitude to what was happening in Algeria which would be consistent with his past and his ideas.

Among other novelists who have depicted the disintegration of the crumbling fabric of French society under the pressures of war and its aftermath are Jean-Louis Curtis and Robert Merle. The latter's *Weekend à Zuydcoote* (1949) is a brilliant account of the retreat to Dunkirk and of the demoralisation of the French army seen through eyes of the soldier Maillat, clear-sighted and disillusioned among the bewilderment and confusion of the battle, the looting and pillage, who saves a girl from being raped and then takes her himself, and later dies in a bombardment. The astringent talents of Merle have been somewhat dissipated in translations (he is an English scholar and an authority on Oscar Wilde), but his next novel, *La Mort est mon métier* (1953), developed the well-worn theme of the concentration camp from the point of view of the oppressor, not the oppressed, analysing the moral weakness of a man who lives by unquestioning obedience to his superiors. Merle is fascinated, like Sartre, by the torments of men pushed to the very limits of their moral strength, and in his latest novel *L'Ile* (1962) he transposes the theme of the Mutiny on the Bounty, substituting noble savages for Cook's flea-ridden Tahitians and setting them up in contrast with a murderous crew of mutineers who take over a Pacific island and gradually decimate themselves with internecine warfare— a topic reminiscent in some ways of *The Lord of the Flies*, with seascapes (particularly the final storm) worthy of Conrad.

Les Forêts de la nuit (1947) by Jean-Louis Curtis, is a chronicle of life in the Basque country and in Paris under the occupation. Less complicated stylistically than Sartre's trilogy which stopped short of the period Curtis treats, the method is one of straightforward realist narrative interspersed with interior monologue and a touch of farce in the depiction of the older generation of provincial bourgeoisie. The book shows the disintegration of the de Balansuns, a middle-class provincial family, under the pressures of the Occupation.

There is a good deal of violence and indignation in Curtis and a final scepticism about the values of the Resistance and the Liberation which seems to declare that the worst have profited from the heroism of the best. This thesis is exploited in *Les Justes Causes* (1954), an exposure of the world of post-war youth for whom these sacrifices were made. *Les Justes Causes* is a by now familiar portrait of an amoral generation, political bigots, careerists, avid of sensation. Its style is rather more complex than the earlier book, in which Curtis showed no scruples about intervening as narrator, as if the advance in this direction had passed him by. In the later work he employs a mixture of styles, showing a great gift for parody, with quotations from diaries, from interviews with real people (there is a good deal of name-dropping), extracts from imaginary plays, etc. In fact there is so much of sheer documentary in Curtis that some of what he writes will date pretty rapidly; but it is precisely the feeling that here is an exact and living representation of post-war France which constitutes his present interest. His latest book, *Cygne sauvage* (1962), returns to the topic of youth, but an idealistic present-day student youth. Technically the book shows some awareness that the art of the novel has not stood still, in its structure of parallel chapters of revelation through dialogue followed by revelation through interior monologue—but perhaps this is little more than a trick to keep in the swim.

The indignation or sadness which lies at the root of most of the literature about the Occupation does not necessarily produce works of art which reflect these moods directly. The same reality has been transposed into one of the most caustically amusing books of the last decade, Jean Dutourd's *Au bon beurre* (1952), a richly farcical account of a dairyman and his wife, Charles-Hubert and Julie Poissonard, who by diligent black-marketing and opportune switches in the correct political attitude not only pass undamaged through the vicissitudes of occupation, resistance, and purges, but end up as millionaires and marry their daughter into the aristocracy,—a Vicar of Bray saga inversely paralleled by the bewildered humiliation of their schoolteacher neighbour, Léon Lécuyer, a latter-day Candide who is buffeted by every change of the political wind and is finally dismissed as a result of the Poissonards' machinations.

The defeat of France was naturally enough seen as a defeat of the older generation which was responsible for it. The familiar need to turn and rend one's predecessors has a ripe savagery in the work of Hervé Bazin which most certainly originates in this disgust with an older France. He is still best known for his early novel *Vipère au poing* (1948) which has no Occupation background but which is clearly born from a similar mood of resentment at the moral and spiritual inadequacy, the moral meanness, of French provincial life. The social stratum of this autobiographical account of childhood is a little higher than that of Curtis: the petty nobility of the Angers region, corseted in pious practices which negate real beliefs, ridiculously obsessed by past grandeurs which have disappeared for ever. The book describes an old-fashioned conflict between a rebellious, ill-treated son and a fantastically exaggerated sadist of a mother, whom he nicknames Folcoche ('Mad-pig'), and who eventually tries to plant a purse of money on her son so that he will be driven out and sent to a remand home; the son having previously connived with his brothers at an attempt first to poison then to drown his mother. The mother is Murdstone-ish in her gruesome unreality, and the concluding sentimentality of the book is disturbing: gradually the son is driven to recognise in his own fierce tenacity the same strength of will that has compelled his mother to

dominate his cowardly father and brothers, a theme which is amplified in the sequel *La Mort du petit cheval* (1950).

The fact that Bazin chooses the Angers area automatically provides a traditional Catholic background to his work, against which his resentment spends itself. But he is not writing in the Catholic tradition in the sense in which, for example, Roger Bésus or Luc Estang consciously attempt to use the moral problems, political, social or artistic, posed by Catholic life in modern France, with its uneasy combination of hidebound tradition and daring experiment. This specifically Catholic literature has a very wide range. Estang himself (*Les Stigmates*, 1949, *Cherchant qui dévorer*, 1951) describes the problems of adolescents undergoing the rigours of a narrowly pietistic education in an environment obsessed with petty morality. The unrelenting exploration of this theme was, naturally enough, repellent to orthodox minds, but Estang's account of the conflicts of young sinners against the background of a church boarding-school is far from being an anti-Catholic book in the sense that *Vipère au poing* is: Estang simply refuses to repeat pious platitudes in a world which has forgotten the reality on which they are based. There is also a fictive world which corresponds to that part of the real world in which, for a time at any rate, the Church approved the initiative of the priest-worker experiment and created at the same time a new figure in the French novel, the unconventional priest of Béatrix Beck's *Léon Morin, prêtre* (1952) and Gilbert Cesbron's *Les Saints vont en enfer* (1952). Cesbron's evocation of a priest working in a depressed urban area among down-and-outs, joining in strikes and peace movements, summoned to withdraw by his Archbishop and having to make the choice between remaining a priest or being a militant worker, suffers too much from its topicality and its close relationship to reportage. His novel on juvenile delinquency, *Chiens perdus sans collier* (1954), shows that his impetus as a novelist, as one might have suspected from *Les Saints vont en enfer*, derives from a documentary rather than an aesthetic appetite. The image of the priest (frequent enough in current French writing) recurs constantly in the work of Roger Bésus. His *Louis Brancourt*

(1955) describes the curious phenomenon of a businessman who feels the pull of the priestly condition and who, in spite of his inability to free himself from a daily sensuality, thinks that in the sacerdotal career lies the best opportunity for what Montherlant has called 'the capture of souls'. In fact Brancourt shows, in the form of a temptation, the possible deformation of the priestly calling. The parallel aberration of a layman is shown in the figure of the novelist Hervé Mauny in *Le Scandale* (1956), who preys on a group of adoring women as a necessary stimulus for his creative talents. The young priest in the book, the abbé Haugard, refuses to accept Mauny's plea that sinning is necessary to be a full man, and that if he is not a full man Mauny cannot write; and if he cannot write he cannot do the good which, it is admitted, his books achieve. Under the pen of a Mauriac or a Graham Greene this could have been a sombre and powerful piece of special pleading; with Bésus, the interest of the argument is there, but the figures are drowned in their own romantic hero-worship which to an English reader seems to verge on the bathetic.

Perhaps inevitably one of the best portraits of the contemporary priest—at least as some envisage his modernity—has been painted 'from the outside'. Béatrix Beck's *Léon Morin, prêtre*, tells the story of Barny (a barely transposed picture of the author in her early novel of the same name) and the attempt to convert her made by an unconventional and tough-minded young priest who meets the vulgarity and crudeness of her world, unshocked, on its own terms. He has the wit and strength to parry Barny's sentimental attachment to him for the sake of the reality of the conversion which he senses beneath it.

Jewish themes in modern French literature, like Catholic ones, often hesitate between the religious and the sociological. At least three novels since the war have treated brilliantly the impact of French life upon the Jewish community. In a style and on a subject which to some readers might recall Louis Golding, Roger Ikor (*Les Fils d'Avrom*, 1955) unfolds over a wide canvas the chronicle of a family of Jewish refugees from Russia in the early years of this century and their slow, difficult, amusing and finally successful insertion into French society, with assimilation and intermarriage as obvious consequential themes. Ikor is a gifted observer and is determinedly not trying to prove anything: 'a novel is not a dissertation' he has, somewhat tritely, declared. Another novel on a similar theme but in a North African setting does appear, on the other hand, to be animated by the desire to prove a case. Albert Memmi's *La Statue de sel* (1953) depicts the contradictions inherent in the situation of a young Jew of Tunis whose language, race, and religion cut him off from the French who occupy his country, and from the Arabs who are its majority. 'A native in a country ruled by settlers, a Jew in an anti-Semitic world, an African in a world where Europe triumphs', he adopts the French language and French civilisation without succeeding in being accepted by the French themselves. It is the process of *Les Fils d'Avrom*, but in reverse, and heading not towards fulfilment but to tragedy.

Neither of these novels has the angry power of André Schwartz-Bart's *Le Dernier des justes* (1959), based on the old legend of the *lamed waf*, the 'just' whose presence God promised to the family of the old rabbi Yom Tov Levy who killed hundreds of the faithful with his own hands to save them from capture and dishonour in the York pogrom of 1185. The history of his family and its 'just man', sacrificed in every generation, is taken through the whole agony of the diaspora up to the timidly courageous figure of Ernie Levy, a refugee from Nazi Germany who goes from Drancy to his death in an Auschwitz gas-chamber. The book has been criticised because of its occasional lapses of style (the author is self-taught) and occasional prolixity; but these weaknesses are negligible beside the emotional drive behind the book, which combines a minute realism of detail and a narrative power with a moving lyricism of unbearable sadness and terror.

The oppression of one race by another has also been reflected in those French novels which spring from the conflict in North Africa. Besides the work of Jules Roy and Emmanuel Roblès, French contemporaries of Camus whose enormous shadow has concealed their very genuine gifts, Morocco and Algeria have produced a number of Arab and Berber writers who use French as their medium in order, paradoxically, to proclaim their separate identity. Many of their novels derive from a simple concern for justice based on the rejection of the economic and social contrasts between the French community and their own, like Mohammed Dib's trilogy *Algérie* (*La Grande Maison*, 1952; *L'Incendie*, 1954; *Le Métier a tisser*, 1957), which has a resonance closely linked to the circumstance which engendered it and, like the work of Curtis, may not survive its passing. Very different is the case of the poet Kateb Yacine's strange novel *Nedjma* (1956), which has been called the best Algerian novel written in French. The surface narration is that of the lives—on and beyond the fringe of crime—of four Algerians in love with the woman Nedjma, herself, like Yacine's art, a product of intercourse between French and Arab, a star round which revolve the planets of the four men, narrating their own stories without any coherent time sequence and always returning to the same central point, Nedjma, as if the progress of the novel were circular and not linear.

That these novels should deal with the disinherited is natural enough. But the disinherited do not live only in North Africa or in the shanty-towns created by the poverty-stricken Algerians in France. They are often the self-deprived that we see in the 'clochard' tradition of the French themselves, the tramps and beggars of Beckett, of the Catholic poet and novelist Jean Cayrol (*Je vivrai l'amour des autres*, 1947–1950), of Jean Genêt's imprisoned homosexuals, murderers, and pimps, and most recently of Jean Cau's *La Pitié de Dieu* (1962), set in a prison cell as claustrophobic as any hell of Sartre's, in which four convicted murderers pass their lives recounting their crimes both real and imaginary, invent games and fantasies, and issue to each other false communiqués about the outside world. Cau had written several novels before this one, and it seems likely that the reason for its success in comparison with the lack of notice achieved by

the others lies in its conformity to a now established tradition of exploration and poetic justification of the underworld of crime and perversion, of 'geekdom', begun by Genêt. He inevitably raises the question, as Beckett does, whether it is necessary to know ultimate degradation to be really confident of rebounding, and also to what extent (in the case of Genêt) the poetry of their creation becomes the justification and redemption of the acts which made it possible.

To a literature long accustomed to the byways of sexual activity, these works are no more than a particular extension of a familiar analysis, which has been handled in a different world and style but with astonishing expertise by Françoise Mallet-Joris in her first novel *Le Rempart des Béguines* (1951) about the Lesbian conquest of a young woman by a masterful and passionate woman much older than herself (a theme with evident echoes of *Huis clos*). In spite of the fact that she was only nineteen when she wrote this novel, her age gave her less magazine popularity than that enjoyed by her contemporary Françoise Sagan (*Bonjour tristesse*, 1954; *Un Certain Sourire*, 1956; *Dans un mois, dans un an*, 1957), whose personal myth and limitations of register should not disguise the fact that she has been able, as perhaps no other present-day writer, to evoke the dry, detached cynicism of her generation, moving in a world of deceptive sexual freedom with an unparalleled capacity for cool cruelty. This in its turn is a world away from the utterly frank and appalling enslavement—sexual and spiritual—of an intelligent woman, by a drunken vagabond who might have stepped straight out of the pages of Genêt, in Christiane Rochefort's *Le Repos du guerrier* (1958).

This survey has omitted much. It has not given any space to what one might call the survivors of the pre-war period. But perhaps enough has been said to show that our attention should not be inordinately distracted, by the technical interest of one sector, from all the other colours of that spectrum which a critic has aptly called 'le roman innombrable'.

G

Some of the distinguished authors published by

Chatto & Windus *and The Hogarth Press*

Lynne Reid Banks	Iris Murdoch
Ann Bridge	*William Plomer*
William Faulkner	*Laurens van der Post*
Sigmund Freud	V. S. Pritchett
David Garnett	Marcel Proust
Henry Green	Fr. Rolfe (Baron Corvo)
Richard Hughes	*William Sansom*
Aldous Huxley	Robert Shaw
Margaret Irwin	Lytton Strachey
Christopher Isherwood	Philip Toynbee
Pär Lagerkvist	Sylvia Townsend Warner
Compton Mackenzie	*Virginia Woolf*

the post-war german novel

by E F GEORGE

Edwin George is a Lecturer in the Department of German of the University of Edinburgh.

In 1945 the German people were confronted with a chaotic situation. Christian and humanist values had been outraged by the Nazis, and although there were many Germans who refused to abandon their principles, the regime had spread its influence throughout the whole of society and corrupted it. It was a question of building new foundations, and this task was made all the more difficult by the feelings of bewilderment and despair which prevailed in Germany as a result of the devastation which she had suffered. Hermann Kasack's *Die Stadt hinter dem Strom*, which was published in 1947, made a considerable impact, because it gave expression to the spirit of the post-war years. Kasack contends that Western civilisation has brought about its own ruin through the one-sided pursuit of technology. It is empty, sterile and incapable of producing new springs of inspiration. Hope lies not in Europe, which has disgraced itself and is exhausted, but in the East, the true and original home of culture and humanity.

Heinrich Böll has to contend with a similar mood of depression. His first two works *Der Zug war pünktlich* (1949) and *Wo warst du, Adam* (1951) give us his picture of the war itself. Pain, discomfort and a sense of complete futility are the dominant impressions which he conveys. Such concepts as military glory and the honour of dying for one's country are in that context seen to be meaningless, or if they have any meaning, they represent a perversion of human values. To die for one's country is to die for Nazi iniquities, for the extermination of the Jews and for the concentration camps with all their fearful apparatus. Men are degraded by the pattern of life into which they are forced. Bravery does not lie in the ability to win medals or in the will to resist: it lies only in the resignation with which soldiers face what they know to be inevitable. Böll's collection of short stories, *Wanderer, kommst du nach Spa* (1950), is in part concerned with the situation after the war. Böll saw that in a society which appears to have fallen apart there can be no sense of security. Fear arises because there is nothing sure in life and because only a very thin and shaky support separates us from despair or annihilation. But to Böll it is also of central importance that this fear should be overcome and that a new confidence in life should be established.

Many writers of the post-war period show themselves to be engaged in a search for values. This was not a new development. It can be traced back to the effects of the 1914–1918 War, when the established order in Europe was overthrown, and to the anxiety which was felt in face of modern life. Kafka may be regarded as a forerunner of what was to come. His works have been related to existentialist philosophy, which has its origins in Kierkegaard and which was developed above all by Heidegger in the nineteen-twenties. Certainly he treats one of the main problems with which the existentialist is concerned, namely the search for reality beneath the artificialities of everyday life.

The basic premise that modern civilisation with its mechanical and soul-destroying implication was leading inevitably to the overthrow of traditional practices, habits and modes of thought was shared by a great number of writers, all of whom started from this assumption and each of whom sought to provide his own solution. Alfred Döblin in *Berlin Alexanderplatz* (1929) proposes an accommodation demanding a readiness for self-sacrifice. Ernst Jünger in his early works advocates submission to the impersonal mechanism of life and even in *Auf den Marmorklippen* (1939) he seems to suggest that civilisations based on humane values must ultimately be destroyed. Kasack sees a solution in a return to eastern pantheism.

Hermann Broch, who emigrated to America in 1938, was convinced that the modern world was destroying the old values which had sustained society, and that man, being left to flounder in a realm devoid of real principles, was seeking a new faith. In Vienna before the last war he became acquainted with the philosophical school of positivism. Being himself a mathematician, he saw its value, but he also recognised its limitations. What he came to seek was a metaphysical explanation of the meaning of life, and this he could not find in the philosophy which was then current in Vienna. His conclusions find expression in *Der Tod des Vergil* (1945). Virgil, who is presented as a dying man, wishes to burn his *Aeneid*, because he feels that his work has been wasted and that he has not fulfilled his true mission as a poet. He has glorified the Roman Empire, instead of conveying to others an insight into ultimate truth. This is an ethical task which must take precedence over all other considerations, and Virgil gains such insight through his approaching encounter with death.

Elisabeth Langgässer was also concerned with the search for meaning and values in life, and the Catholicism in which she found her solution has often been considered to have an existentialist tinge. She was very conscious of the evil forces active in the world, and this led her to dwell in her writing on manifestations of human depravity. In *Das unauslöschliche Siegel* (1946) the conflict between good and evil is treated in theological terms, and the question arises as to how man can be redeemed. The indelible seal to which the title refers is the seal of baptism. Elisabeth Langgässer suggests that Satan's power lies not only in the wickedness which he engenders, but also in a nihilistic approach to life, and that the only way in which he can be overcome is by trusting in God and basing one's whole life upon this trust, even though there can be no convincing proof that such a God exists. It is a question not of understanding but of blind faith.

Stefan Andres does not take such a sombre view of human nature as Elisabeth Langgässer. He combines a firm faith in God with much that has been taken over from the humanist tradition. This enables him, while taking into account the destructive tendencies of the age, the upheavals, the violence and the suffering, to perceive nevertheless a basis of order and a spiritual strength within man which has an ennobling influence. His novel *Ritter der Gerechtigkeit* (1948) is concerned with the need to find the right principles on which to act in conditions of chaos and confusion. The scene is set in Naples and the surrounding district in summer 1943, a time when Fascism was in the process of collapsing. The great majority of people are shown to have lost their bearings. Many of them are opportunists who seek to do whatever suits their advantage. But against this background are set certain individuals who refuse to conform to such an attitude and who seek to bring standards of justice into their lives.

After the currency reform in 1948 conditions in Germany showed a remarkable improvement, but for some years many people had to contend with hardships. There was a housing shortage, and although food became much more plentiful and luxury articles began to appear, there was a strange mixture of ruins and reconstruction, of wealth in some circles and of want and deprivation in others. It is with this situation that Böll is concerned in his novels *Und sagte kein einziges Wort* (1953) and *Haus ohne Hüter* (1954). In both cases marriage and family life are the main themes. He shows the ways in which they may be disrupted and he points to the need for cohesion. Here his Catholicism emerges. It is for him a question of moral and religious principle, but this cannot be separated from such considerations as the love and trust between husband and wife, the care and upbringing of children, and the health of society as a whole. As prosperity developed, Böll complained that worldly possessions, a lucrative job and a good bank balance were the aims encouraged by modern society. In *Das Brot der frühen Jahre* (1955) he puts in a protest against the prevailing materialistic outlook, but he also presents it as a problem which is not capable of easy solution.

Mention must be made of two Austrian writers of outstanding significance, whose works, although concerned with the social scene of an earlier day, reflect an attitude of mind which is relevant to modern developments. Robert Musil in *Der Mann ohne Eigenschaften*, which was published in its final form in 1952 (he himself died in 1942), centres his interest around the reflections and reactions to life of his hero, Ulrich, who resides in Vienna in the year preceding the 1914–18 War. Ulrich is a man without qualities, because he is unattached to any moral, social or philosophical principles. He endeavours to find an aim in life and work which will satisfy his demands, but in this he fails. The social circumstances in which he lives are precarious, and the collapse, which is foreshadowed in the unhealthy state of society, finally comes with the outbreak of war. Heimito von Doderer also depicts Viennese society, and like Musil he examines the underlying malaise. *Die Dämonen* (1956) deals with events in the lives of a wide variety of people, seen chiefly from the point of view of the narrator, Geyrenhoff, who had been an official in the Austrian civil service but has now retired at an unusually early age. The period covered is short, from autumn 1926 to July 15th 1927, a precise date, because it was then that social unrest reached a climax and the Palace of Justice was burnt down. Doderer calls this the 'Cannae' of Austrian democracy, because it clearly demonstrated the disregard of political parties for the rule of law. It is regarded as the inevitable outcome of the kind of conditions and outlook which have been carefully described, and it opens up the prospect of further disruption and chaos.

Some German writers have felt the need to depart from the traditional narrative form of the novel. Döblin in *Berlin Alexanderplatz* leads the way here. The life of a great industrial city with all its bustle and turmoil is conveyed through fragmentary impressions, apparently unconnected but in reality skilfully interwoven. The experiences of the hero are seen from within through his instinctive reactions, and the perspectives are constantly shifting. Broch in *Der Tod des Vergil* analyses Virgil's mental struggles in the form of an inner monologue. Elisabeth Langgässer rebelled against the tyranny of a closely knit plot. In place of this she preferred a theme which could be illuminated from different points of view. As a novelist she did not consider herself bound by continuity either in time or in place. Böll, being concerned with social criticism, takes us through his characters into the routine of life as it is lived from day to day. In *Und sagte kein einziges Wort* he presents the situation through the eyes of both husband and wife, so that the two perspectives complement each other. Gerd Gaiser in *Schluß-ball* (1958) goes a stage further than this. The voices of a group of characters are heard reviewing their own positions: these are, Gaiser writes, interacting voices, none of which speaks to the others but each of which speaks of himself and for himself alone. But when taken together, they disclose the tangle of thoughts and emotions which spring from the conditions of a modern community.

It would be surprising if the modern German novel failed to express the ever-present awareness that Germany is divided into two states, one of which is governed in accordance with Western democratic principles and the other subjected to Communist rule. Germany's position is unenviable, not only because the conflict between two opposing political systems is manifested here in a most acute form, but because in many cases personal issues are involved. Uwe Johnson has been acclaimed as a writer of distinction to whom credit is due for having treated the problems and perplexities of this basic situation. He came over to the West in 1959 and his novel *Mutmaßungen über Jakob* was published in that same year. Since then his reputation has been confirmed by the recent publication of a second novel *Das dritte Buch über Achim*. Uwe Johnson is balanced in his judgments. He penetrates deeply into the theme of what he calls the frontier, the difference and the distance, and this he does with a flexible and varied use of language and with structural methods which enable him to move freely from one position to another.

Norman Mailer

Poems, *Deaths for the Ladies (and Other Disasters)* (12/6) coming soon. Author of *Advertisements for Myself* (21/-), *The Naked and the Dead* (12/6), *The Deer Park* (15/-).

John Updike

Author of the novel *Rabbit, Run* (16/-) and stories, *The Same Door* (16/-). *Pigeon Feathers* coming soon.

Richard Yates

Author of *Revolutionary Road* (18/-). Stories, *Eleven Kinds of Loneliness* (18/-), coming early next year.

Roy Fuller

Collected Poems (25/-) just out. Author of novels *The Father's Comedy* (13/6), *The Ruined Boys* (15/-), *Image of a Society* (13/6), *Fantasy and Fugue* (6/-) and *Second Curtain* (5/-).

Philip Roth

His second novel, *Letting Go* (25/-), coming soon. It's already on the best-seller list in the U.S.A.

Otto F. Walter

His first novel, *The Mute* (18/-), coming soon, translated from the German by Michael Bullock.

Brian Moore

A novel, *An Answer from Limbo* (16/-), coming early next year. Author of *The Luck of Ginger Coffey* (15/-). He also wrote *Judith Hearne* and *The Feast of Lupercal*.

Jack Kerouac

Lonesome Traveller (15/-) just out. Author of *On the Road*, *The Dharma Bums* (15/- each) and *The Subterraneans* (10/6).

V. S. Naipaul

The Middle Passage (25/-), a book on the Caribbean, just out. Author of *A House for Mr Biswas* (21/-), *The Mystic Masseur*, *Miguel Street* (15/- each).

Edmund Wilson

Patriotic Gore (55/-) just out. This 'rich and splendid' book (BBC Critics) is a study of the literature of the American Civil War.

ANDRE DEUTSCH

 We would be pleased to put you on our mailing list. Write to us at 105 Great Russell Street, London WC1

contemporary indian writing in english

by KHUSHWANT SINGH

Khushwant Singh has worked for the Indian government and for UNESCO. He is at present engaged on a history of the Sikhs, commissioned by the Rockefeller Foundation. His publications include the novels 'Train to Pakistan' (1954) and 'I shall not hear the Nightingale' (1961).

The Indian constitution recognises fourteen major languages including English. Although every one of the other thirteen is spoken by a larger number of people, English is the only medium of communication between people of different linguistic groups. The debates of the two Houses of the Indian Parliament and the State Assemblies are largely conducted in English. More newspapers and journals are published in English than in any of the Indian languages and the English press enjoys greater prestige than the vernacular. Indians often boast that next to the English, Irish, and the Americans whose mother tongue it is, they speak and write the English language better than any other people in the world. Despite all this, the Indian attitude towards English is, and always has been, one of reserve as towards an alien language. It *was* the most effective means of propaganda against the British Raj and *is* today necessary for acquiring technical knowledge. Its lease is reluctantly renewed every few years while Hindi is being tutored to take its place. Indians stubbornly refused to cultivate an affection for English. Those who fell victim to its charms seldom did more than read good literature. They did not feel that they should write novels or poems in English. This attitude prevented them from producing anything worthwhile and is the chief reason why Indo-Anglian writing, as it is often called, has remained utterly second-rate. Whereas South Africa and the West Indies (two of whose distinguished novelists, Naipaul and Selvom, are of Indian origin) have produced distinct schools of English writing, India's contribution to English literature has been of little significance.

The Indian climate continues to be adverse to the writer of English. An example of this is the attitude of the Sahitya Akademi—an officially sponsored academy of letters established in 1952. One of the functions of this body is to select the best work of prose or poetry of each of the fourteen languages produced in the year. The President of the Republic honours the author or the poet by giving him an award of Rs. 5000 (£375). In the last ten years sixty-eight writers of Indian languages have won these awards. The only writer of English to have made the grade is R. K. Narayan who was honoured last year for his novel *The Guide*. Neither the poet, Dom Moraes, who won the Hawthornden prize for poetry, nor the essayist Nirad C. Chaudhuri (*Autobiography of an Unknown Indian* and *Passage to England*), nor the novelist Bala Chandra Rajan whose *The Dark Dancer* became a Book Society choice, nor even Kamala Markandaya, whose *Nectar in a Sieve* is the most widely read English novel in India—all of whom are rated higher than most of their vernacular-writing compatriots—has been considered fit to be so honoured. The Sahitya Akademi reflects the attitude of the Government in believing that Indian languages need to be encouraged; English does not. English has no place in the officially inspired literary renaissance that is taking place in the country. The Indian writer of English has always been and is likely to remain an outcast in his own homeland.

The most important result of this attitude is that few Indians have really bothered to take trouble with the English language. Basic literature like the Bible, folk-lore, nursery rhymes, nonsense verse, etc., does not form a part of the school curriculum and is therefore seldom read by Indians. Even in homes where English was spoken, it remained as it does today, a second language, borrowing its similes, metaphors, imagery and frequently even the grammatical construction from the vernacular. This Hobson Jobson can be amusing but seldom, if ever, literary. A Punjabi clerk flaunting a B.A.(Hons.)Eng.Lit. on his visiting card may welcome you with the following address: 'Please do feel at home, we are all in the family way'.

A direct consequence of the neglect of English is the extremely limited vocabulary of English words in the repertoire of most Indian writers. Some antiquities continue to be sold as new and clichés are rated high. Small shops describe themselves as Emporiums or marts; if they sell medicine, they will be known as 'Medical Halls'. Large houses have 'compounds'. Civil servants on tour are 'out of station'. Politicians address meetings in halls 'packed to capacity' and are heard in 'pin-drop silence'; they exhort their audience to 'eschew' this or that and 'sacrifice their all' to the motherland. For their advice they often get pelted with 'brickbats'. In Army officers' messes where everything is 'tickety boo', Colonel Singh downs his Scotch and soda with the same words that the English subaltern in the service of the 'Company Sahib Bahadur' used before the Great Mutiny of 1857. In India English is not a living language. It died in the time of Malika Victoria and has been preserved in its Victorian state embalmed in oriental spices.

Interest in nature is somewhat alien to the Indian temperament. Few Indians bother themselves with names of birds, trees, or wild flowers (that is dismissed as an English affectation, the *snobisme anglais*). Consequently India, which is one of the most photogenic countries of the world, remains largely unknown. Kipling and Edward Thompson made a few uninspiring attempts to portray it; but no Indian has ever essayed it; he simply does not know the names of the flora and fauna.

The biggest problem facing the Indian writer of English is that of his audience. For reasons already stated, and the fact that publishing in India is still economically unsound, he has to find a publisher abroad. In India itself an English novel published in Bombay or Calcutta does not have the prestige that it would have if it were published in London or New York. A favourable review in the *Observer* or the *New Statesman* is worth more than notices in all the Indian papers put together. For an Indian to arrive in Delhi he has to take the bus to Fleet Street and not a tonga to the Grand Trunk Road. It is not surprising that Indian novelists are unhealthily conscious of their foreign readership and often give their works the semblance of a tourist guide. The passion with which they describe family customs, festivals, and the food they eat is usually to tell the reader 'something about India'. Ruth Jhabvala, the leading woman novelist of the country, took the easier course of publishing recipes of Indian curries as an appendix to her first novel.

Who are the Indian writers and poets that Indians themselves rate high? Rabindra Nath Tagore's and Sarojini Naidu's poems had a great vogue twenty years ago (Tagore's birth centenary has revived interest in his works). Dr. Radhakrishnan, President of the Republic, and Krishnamurthy, the reluctant avatar, are highly respected as exponents of Indian religious philosophy. Pandit Nehru's autobiography shares with the translation of the *Bhagavadagita* and the *Kama Sutra* (Hindi art of love) the top place as India's best seller. And Nirad C. Chaudhuri whose views on his country and countrymen are fiercely resented by his compatriots is conceded the place of honour as the best writer of English prose in India today. The praise bestowed on Radhakrishnan, Nehru, or Nirad Chaudhuri is not extended to the novelists—and that for good reason.

Up till 1947, most Indian writers used fiction to sugar-coat anti-Raj propaganda pills. The two leading writers of this school of socio-political writers were Mulk Raj Anand and Raja Rao. After independence, the political leitmotiv virtually disappeared and a new story-for-story's-sake school of writers who turned to the portrayal of Indian life and character came up. Prominent writers of this school are R. K. Narayan (*The Guide*, *Financial Expert*, etc.), Bhabani Bhattacharya (*Of So Many Hungers*, *He Who Rides a Tiger*, etc.), Sudhin Ghose (*Vermilion Boat*, *Cradle in the Clouds*, *Flame of the Forest*, etc.), Bal Chandra Rajan and Govind Desani (*All about H. Hatterr*) and a group of distinguished women: Ruth Jhabvala, Santha Rama Rau, Kamala Markandaya, Nain Tara Sehgal, and Atia Hussain. The first school made some contribution towards informing the British public of the Indian point of view in the struggle for freedom but (with the exception of Raja Rao's *Kanthapura*)

did little more. The emotions of the writers were so involved in their themes that instead of being ironic they were angry, and instead of drawing their characters with a fine brush they caricatured them with a blunt reed pen.

The Indian novel in English came into its own with R. K. Narayan. He is the most successful of Indian novelists writing in English and without any question, the dominant figure of the contemporary literary scene. Narayan is essentially a spinner of stories and as unpretentious in his writing as he is in his mode of living. There is a quality of naïveté in the language he uses which endears him to foreigners. He has a dry but kindly sense of humour which make his characters lovable. Although none of Narayan's characters stay too long in the reader's mind, he has succeeded in putting the town of Malgudi, the location of most of his stories, on the literary map of India. His two best works are *The Financial Expert* and *The Guide*.

Narayan's influence can be discerned in the writings of many of his younger contemporaries, who like him choose the rustic theme and try to imitate his simple English. Most of this imitation is deliberate and stems from the belief that Narayan succeeds because he writes the sort of thing that is expected from an Indian. And since the eyes of these imitators are fixed on the reader, their pens take a wayward course across the paper.

THE FUTURE

In the last fifteen years, standards of English in India have been getting lower and lower. In many colleges new entrants have to be put through a short course in spoken English to enable them to follow the lectures. The Government no longer allows foreign exchange for the study of humanities in universities abroad; the number of Indians studying English literature in British or American universities can now be counted on one's fingers. In short, English is fast being reduced to a language of communication and deprived of its creative potential. In these circumstances, India is no more likely than France or Italy to produce a great poet or novelist writing in English.

LAWRENCE DURRELL

<u>WORKS IN PRINT</u>:—FICTION—Justine, Balthazar, Mountolive, Clea (The Alexandria Quartet); The Dark Labyrinth. TRAVEL — Bitter Lemons, Reflections on a Marine Venus, Prospero's Cell. POETRY — Collected Poems, Selected Poems, The Tree of Idleness, On Seeming to Presume. DRAMA — Sappho, Acte (in preparation), Faustus (in preparation).

WILLIAM GOLDING

<u>WORKS IN PRINT</u>: — FICTION — Lord of the Flies, The Inheritors, Pincher Martin, Free Fall. DRAMA — The Brass Butterfly.

NEIL M. GUNN

<u>WORKS IN PRINT</u>: — FICTION — The Other Landscape, Young Art and Old Hector, The Well at the World's End, The Silver Darlings, Morning Tide, The White Hour, The Lost Chart, The Silver Bough, The Drinking Well, The Green Isle of the Great Deep, Highland Pack.

FABER AND FABER LIMITED

the contemporary italian novel

by KATHLEEN SPEIGHT

Dr. Speight is Senior Lecturer in Italian Studies at the University of Manchester.

The poet Giosuè Carducci (1835–1907) once said that the Italian genuis was unsuited to the novel; and as recently as some thirty years ago the question was hotly debated by critics. Today the picture is completely changed. Since the war, with the fall of the Fascist dictatorship and consequent freedom from restraint, there has been a flood of Italian writings of all kinds, particularly of narrative works; and among these, many novels have earned the distinction of being translated. To instance only a few, the names of Moravia, Carlo Levi, Vittorini, Pratolini, Guareschi, and Elsa Morante are all familiar to our novel-reading public. With such a wealth of production it is not possible to do more here than indicate some of the main characteristics of these writers, and many names must perforce be passed by.

A survey is made more difficult by the fact that Italy, having achieved national unity comparatively late, has no one main cultural centre. This makes for independence of outlook and greater variety, but means lack of a single standard of taste and achievement, and of a common cultural and social background favourable to the growth of a national tradition for the novel. It also leads to 'provincialism'. Sometimes charged with being 'provincial', in the sense of being limited in intellectual interests and as regards form and technique, Italian novelists, compared in their technique with that of Henry James, Proust, Joyce, Virginia Woolf, and in intellectual interests and the solution of problems with Thomas Mann, Aldous Huxley, or André Gide, do seem somewhat outside the general European development, except for a few cases, such as that of Pirandello, Svevo, or Moravia. In the etymological sense, Italian authors *are* provincial: Alvaro immediately recalls Calabria; Vittorini, Sicily; Pavese, Piedmont; Cassola, the Maremma; for in Italy, the province is the reality. Similarly, the Italian language is not unified (though modern ways of life are hastening the process of standardisation); and the Italian of a Svevo from Trieste differs from that of a Pratolini, a Florentine; or of L. Sciascia, a Sicilian; or of G. Dessí, a Sardinian; while some novelists present their environment realistically by using dialect, as Pasolini in his novels of the slum life of boys in the Roman suburbs, *Ragazzi di vita* (1955) and *Una vita violenta* (1959); and in C. E. Gadda's *Quer pasticciaccio di via Merulana* (1957) three dialects—Venetian, Neapolitan, and Roman—are necessary for the meaning, as well as to produce the comic and grotesque effects. It is interesting to note that this last, a detective story dealing with a robbery in the streets of Rome and involving a large number of people, is in atmosphere very similar to that of neo-realist films, such as *Open City* and *Paisà*.

Italian novelists sometimes look to foreign models: to Joyce, Proust, and surrealism; to Faulkner and Hemingway, as may be seen in Vittorini and Pavese; and, more recently, to Pasternak, whose *Dr. Zhivago* has left traces in Carlo Cassola's *Fausto e Anna* (1958). But neo-realism, the tendency to which nearly all novelists in greater or lesser degree belong, has been called a 'return to Verga' (1840–1922), in whom are certain characteristics, which recur, with modifications, in the present day. These are: truthful representation of a particular aspect of reality (as an observer, not a judge); a tendency to find inspiration in the life of a particular region, usually that of the poorer classes; and an effort to get closer to the people by the use of their language. Verga's *I Malavoglia* (1881, new edition of translation 1950) is an epic story of the unequal struggle of humble Sicilian fisher-folk against social, economic, and natural forces. A faithful picture of their lives is given objectively in a style and language intimately fused with the content and the characters. Events are reported as briefly as possible; there is little formal description or narrative, much of the story being told through the dialogue, which is written in an Italian which seems to echo Sicilian in its phrases and intonation, conciseness, and simplicity. The characteristics of this dialogue extend to the narrative, till narration and dialogue are hardly distinguishable, and the fishermen themselves seem to be telling the story.

Elio Vittorini, also Sicilian, owes much to his great predecessor. Of the older generation, he proclaimed that Italian literature should deal realistically with social problems, and his *Conversazione in Sicilia* (1936, published 1941, translated 1948) is one of the earliest neo-realist works. His Sicily of today is true to life and crude in its reality; his style is aggressive, polemical; his language sometimes brutal and violent. The meaning of the book is not in the few facts related baldly, but in the value the author gives to them. Written during the 'black' twenty years, his journey into Sicily is as a journey to another world, primitive, innocent, pure; the symbol of his search for sincerity, truth, and faith. Cesare Pavese, Piedmontese (1908–50), a contemporary of Vittorini, is considered with him as a master, by the younger generation. The preoccupation of Pavese with political and social themes is seen in *Carcere* (1938), in which he studies and denounces the attitude of passive indifference to Fascism of the intellectuals; and in *Paesi tuoi* (1941), which attacks the conventions and conformism of the lower middle classes, with their compromises, imposed by persons of mediocre mentality and without moral fibre. His best work, *La luna e i falò* (1950, translated 1952), a short novel of great lyrical beauty, is the story of the return from America of a poor waif (now with a fortune) to his village in Piedmont; of his joy in seeing his native place again; of sorrow in finding so many things altered; only one friend is left, Nuto, the player of the clarinet in the village band. The story of his contemporaries unfolds in his conversation with Nuto. The style is simple, straightforward, even curt. When relating highly dramatic or tragic events, or something which moves him deeply, his prose is always calm, even, without any raising of voice, a slow-moving monotone. This type of prose had great influence on the younger generation, as is evident, for example, in the *Storie ferraresi* (1955–60) and *Gli occhiali d' oro* (1958, translated 1960) by Giorgio Bassani, told with the same calm composure; and particularly in the work of another Piedmontese, Natalia Ginsburg, in her latest short novel, *Le voci della sera* (1961), a masterpiece of its kind. With its quiet subdued title, it is a story about quiet, modest, rather apathetic people, told soberly, without any comment, opinions, or introspection.

Books based on war experiences also partake of some of these characteristics. Giuseppe Berto's *Il cielo è rosso* (1947, translated 1949) is one of the most significant. An impressive account of war set against the background of a bombed city, it brings out the dramatic contrast between conqueror and conquered, between the poor and destitute and the rich (still selfishly eager to protect their property). The story of four teenage orphans, their struggle for existence in dreadful misery and squalor and their tragic end, serves to emphasise the wickedness of war, and to point to an innate goodness in the human character, which develops under the impact of great suffering. Of many others inspired by war, such as G. Petroni's *Il mondo é una prigione* (1949), M. Tobino's *Il deserto della Libia* (1952) and Renata Viganò's *Agnese va a morire* (1954), *La Ciociara* (1957, translated 1960) by Alberto Moravia should be specially noted. Of contemporary novelists, Moravia is probably the best known abroad and is one of the most prolific writers. The book tells the story of two evacuees; and although his vision is somewhat distorted by his obsession with sex, here too is apparent a fundamental goodness in human nature, seen particularly in the patience and stoicism of the ordinary people.

With the transformation of the political and social scene after the war and the realisation of the state of moral decadence reached under Fascism, the novelist assumed more than ever before a moral responsibility before his public. Social, political, and moral problems loom large in neo-realist writers, such as Vittorini, Pratolini, F. Jovine, and G. Petroni. Some novelists had anticipated this trend. Moravia, in his first novel, *Gli indifferenti* (1929) implied a condemnation of a corrupt and idle social class; so utterly worthless and objectionable did he make them. They may be taken as representing the apathy and moral disintegration of a class which had been content to endure Fascism. But this is only implied; the author's attitude is analytical and submissive, rather than critical. In a way Moravia anticipates existentialism. He is neo-realist; but with a cold, pitiless attitude towards his characters, nearer to 'naturalism' than to Italian 'realism' and Verga. A change has been noted, however, in his latest novel, *La noia* (1961, translated as 'The Empty Canvas', 1962), where he is said to have more the compassionate eye of a doctor who wishes to effect a cure, rather than his usual cold, inhuman, documentary eye of the chronicler.

The moral responsibility of the novelist is nowhere more evident than in the works of Ignazio Silone, whose early novels, written in exile, only became known to the Italian public after the liberation; and until recently he has not had the honour due to him from his countrymen. His latest work, *La volpe e le camellie* (1960) was, however, well received; but he has remained a rather isolated figure and outside the general trends in Italy. In content, and in the spirit of his work, the nearest to him is perhaps Carlo Levi, in *Cristo si è fermato a Eboli* (1945, translated 1948). This work awakened the Italians to the bitter realisation of the tragic conditions of life in the impoverished and backward south; and was the first of a series of works, partly narrative, partly documentary, dealing with this vast problem. Francesco Jovine's *Le terre del sacramento* (1950, translated 1952) takes for its main theme the struggle between farm labourers and tyrannical landowners in the Molise at the beginning of the Fascist period in 1922. Highly satirical, it gives a vivid and realistic picture of the south of Italy and of its people and problems at that time; while Rocco Scotellaro's *Contadini del sud* (1954), more documentary than narrative, is one of the most interesting of these works, as being written by one who is of peasant stock. The book takes the form of interviews with various country folk; and the simple, stark, language of their replies heightens the pathos of the sadness and loneliness of their lives.

A neo-realist tendency is to study life collectively rather than life in the individual; to study the aims and hopes of a group rather than analyse a character. Carlo Bernari's *Tre operai* (1934), a story of the working-class movement at the beginning of the century (but symbolical of the hopelessness of the condition of the working classes under the dictatorship), may be taken as anticipating this trend. Of the younger generation, Vasco Pratolini is its main exponent in *Il quartiere* (1944, translated 1948) and *Cronaca di poveri amanti* (1947, translated 1948), depicting life in the poor quarters near Santa Croce in Florence. His main theme, the class struggle and hope for betterment for the masses, is the basis of his latest work, a trilogy, *Una storia italiana*, of which two parts, *Metello* and *Lo scialo* (1955-60) are complete; and in which he presents, in the story of a bricklayer, the history of the working-class movement in Florence.

Three women novelists are introspective-realists, rather than neo-realists: Anna Banti, who studies the position of women in society in her *Artimisia* (1950); Elsa Morante, who in *Isola di Arturo* (1958, translated 1959) presents a study of the childhood and youth of a motherless boy and his initiation into the mysteries of good and evil; and Fausta Cialente, whose *Ballata levantina* (1961) is a story, very well told, of the European community in Egypt before the war. An ironical attitude towards the mechanisation of our modern life is expressed in Italo Calvino's fantastic and humorous novels, such as *Il barone rampante* (1957); while the Mafia is dealt with in a masterly story by L. Sciascia, a Sicilian, in his first novel, *Il giorno della civetta* (1961). But Italy often springs surprises. In 1958, Giuseppe Tomasi di Lampedusa's historical novel *Gattopardo* (translated 1960) was wildly acclaimed as a best seller, and as perhaps foreshadowing a return to some traditional kind of novel. And, curiously, another historical novel was being written about the same time. Silvio D'Amico's *Le finestre di Piazza Navona* (1961, posthumous), like *Gattopardo* is written in a spirit and in a style more reminiscent of last century than of our own day.

Both novels, with their interest in character, have appeared at a moment when neo-realism seems to be giving way to a new 'human realism', noted in some younger writers, as M. Prisco, C. Cassieri, M. Franciosa; and in Bassani's *Il giardino dei Finzi-Contini* (1961), with its affectionate evocation of a community and an epoch, and of the wayward and attractive Micol. But most of all this 'human' realism is seen in *La ragazza di Bube* (1960, translated 1961), in Cassola's study of Mara, the lively and, apparently, thoughtless and careless young woman of the people, whose love for Bube becomes a thing of beauty, and in whom sorrow only serves to strengthen the moral fibre. It is a realism characterised by a return to the world of feeling and affection, to a more confident faith in human destiny, and to a more positive and hopeful humanity as opposed to the negations of the existentialists and to the resigned despair of neo-realism.

the post-war russian novel

by RONALD HINGLEY

Ronald Hingley is University Lecturer in Russian and Research Fellow of St. Antony's College, Oxford. His books on Russia, Russian literature and language, include 'Chekhov', 'Soviet Prose', 'Under Soviet Skins' and 'The Undiscovered Dostoyevsky'.

Soviet writings present the spectacle of a literature closely controlled by officials in the interests of what are, to most people other than sympathisers of Communism, non-literary aims. It would therefore be very difficult to approach the subject of the contemporary Russian novel from an aesthetic point of view such as can be taken when considering the literature of a free society, and it is in any case doubtful whether such an approach would lead to very interesting conclusions.

This is particularly true of the immediate post-war period—more exactly of the period between 1946 and the death of Stalin in 1953. Of all phases of Soviet literature this was the one in which the hand of officialdom lay most heavily on the writers, who, according to temperament or luck, lapsed into silence, were imprisoned or executed, denounced others or were themselves denounced. This is usually called the 'Zhdanov period' after the cultural dictator Andrey Zhdanov, whose style of control continued to operate after his death in 1948.

Surprisingly enough, the Russian novel did not die under these conditions. In fact it flourished, at least from a quantitative point of view. Russian novels have always been lengthy. They now became longer still, owing to the widespread fashion amongst established writers of producing 'trilogies' of novels tracing the fortunes of the same group of characters over a fairly long period of time. Such trilogies or sequences of novels, were produced by Kaverin, Panfyorov, and many others. The most important is that of Fedin—the three novels *Early Joys*, *An Unusual Summer*, and *The Bonfire*. On the whole, however, this is stodgy stuff, of some technical interest to the student of the Soviet scene, but with little to offer the general reader.

Of post-war novels by established Soviet novelists the most interesting is one which does not belong to a trilogy—Leonov's long novel, *The Russian Forest*. This was written during Stalin's lifetime and published shortly after his death. Like all Leonov's work it is an extremely subtle and complicated piece of writing which requires thoughtful assimilation. The subject perhaps sounds odd to those unacquainted with the Soviet novel, since it depicts a protracted duel between two professors of forestry, the one a sincere student with the interests of the Russian forest at heart, the other a careerist and intriguer. The work is an allegory in which Russian trees are symbolic of Russian people, and under this disguise Leonov was able to develop a criticism of Stalinist practice which was astonishingly daring considering the conditions of the time.

Of other previously established novelists Sholokhov has produced the most disappointing performance. His pre-war *Quiet Don* is the supreme masterpiece of Soviet prose, revealing him as a master of turbulent narrative and character-drawing, and also as an original stylist. For over twenty years readers, not only in Russia, have been waiting for Sholokhov to repeat this performance, but in vain. The only work of any length to have come from his pen since *The Quiet Don* is the second volume of his novel of collectivisation, *Virgin Soil Upturned*. This is an amusing and lively work, but it is a string of episodes rather than a novel, and its approach to the problems of the Russian countryside seems to be basically frivolous.

Sholokhov has also produced a war story called *They Fought for their Country*, which he has sub-titled 'chapters from a novel'. Broadly speaking, this suffers from the same faults as *Virgin Soil Upturned*, and it begins to seem as if he is unlikely to recover his touch.

Novels about the Second World War are continuing to appear, and one reason for this is that Soviet writers now enjoy relative freedom to describe the war as they saw it. One of the best among such recent works is Simonov's *The Living and the Dead*, which represents a considerable improvement on his earlier novel of Stalingrad, *Days and Nights*. Stalingrad, incidentally, is the scene of one of the best Soviet war novels, Nekrasov's *Front-Line Stalingrad*, which has just appeared in English translation. One other war novel must be mentioned here, if only because of its strange fate. This is Fadeyev's *Young Guard*, which deals with the partisan movement amongst young Russians. The novel first appeared in 1945, but it was soon discovered that Fadeyev had committed the political crime of under-estimating the controlling role of the Communist party under wartime conditions. He had to spend four years re-writing the novel. There would be nothing extraordinary about the incident were it not for the fact that Fadeyev was himself the leading official of the Writer's Union, and was more used to the rôle of ordering other writers about than of being told what to do himself.

The Zhdanov period was not a favourable time for the appearance of new novelists, but new names did of course appear. The most important was probably Vera Panova, who was continually getting into trouble for depicting Soviet humanity as more complicated than official theory allowed. Her novels, rather short by Russian standards, vary in interest according to the degree to which she was under attack. One of the best is *The Seasons of the Year*, in which a relatively frank account is given of the seamier sides of Soviet life.

One of the most important Soviet writers during the post-war period as a whole is Ilya Ehrenburg, who is in fact a very poor novelist, since he suffers from the inability to create either convincing characters or strong plots. His novels are really an extension of his journalism, and their interest derives from his wide experience of intellectual life, both in the West and in Russia, his skill in adapting himself to changing conditions of control, and his function as a 'barometer' of the Soviet intellectual climate.

Before and during the Zhdanov period Ehrenburg produced a vast and tedious trilogy (*The Fall of Paris*, *The Storm*, and *The Ninth Wave*). But it was Ehrenburg who marked the change away from the gross illiberalism of Stalin to the relatively mild illiberalism of Khrushchev, and who incidentally gave a name to the post-Zhdanov era, with his short novel *The Thaw*. This is sufficiently well known in England, and it is of course a very poor novel. Under Soviet conditions, however, its appearance was dramatic, because it discussed topics hitherto taboo—admittedly in a remote and allusive fashion. These included the concentration camps, Soviet anti-Semitism (and the associated notorious 'doctors' plot') and the deadening effect of Soviet controls over the arts. Since then the interest of Ehrenburg's writings has switched to memoirs and essays, which continue to provide valuable barometric readings.

Opinions vary as to the suitability of 'thaw' as a metaphor to cover post-Stalinist Soviet cultural developments. No one doubts that there has been a great rise in temperature since the deep freeze of earlier days, but there is still more slush than sunshine to be observed in the cultural landscape. The temperature varies according to the periodical switches of cultural policy from cool to tepid, and as is well known the year of greatest warmth was 1956. This was the year of Dudintsev's celebrated novel *Not by Bread Alone*, again a work with which the West is familiar. This was more notable for its frontal assault on the entrenched Soviet 'Establishment' than for its literary qualities, though these are not entirely negligible. Actually *Not by Bread Alone* is only one among a number of recent Soviet managerial novels (the Russian equivalent of C. P. Snow), which now began to appear. It was the most outspoken of all and for this reason attracted most attention, but there are many others which repay attention — for instance, Granin's *Seekers*. It was now possible, still within limits which free societies would regard as rigid, to criticise Soviet conditions, but on the whole this has found expression in poetry, essays, and short stories rather than in novels.

We now approach a period which may be said to have begun about 1958, in which Soviet writers increasingly range themselves into two opposing camps, most conveniently termed Soft and Hard. The Hards are those who support a tough line on literature, whereas the Softs are those who want greater freedom for the writers. On the whole it is the Hards who write novels, whereas the Softs prefer poetry (like Tvardovsky and Yevtushenko) or have reverted to memoirs (like Paustovsky and Ehrenburg). The chief Hard spokesman at the moment is the editor and novelist Kochetov, who presents a phenomenon of great interest. His most recent novel, *The Secretary of the District Committee*, may not be a great work of art, but it makes absorbing reading. It aroused a storm of criticism in the Soft press, where Kochetov was accused, not without reason, of hankering after the bad old days of Stalin. This, as the title indicates, is another 'managerial' novel.

One of the most common battle-cries of the Hards is the clamour for what they call 'contemporaneity'. They want novelists to show Soviet workers, peasants and intellectuals battling together to create the new society—in other words, they want to turn novelists into advertising copy-writers. The Softs, on the other hand, have evolved the so-called 'theory of distance' whereby a writer is thought to be able to write more effectively about events from which he is removed in time. Among such writers a nostalgia has grown up for Russia of the 'twenties, now a favourite topic, which appears, for example, in Nilin's excellent short novel *Cruelty*.

In general it may be said that the Soviet novel, whether written by Hards or Softs, suffers from the curse of didacticism. Whether they write advertising copy or criticise existing conditions, Soviet writers are concerned to teach more directly than has usually been found consistent with the production of work with a high literary value, as this is understood in the West. On the whole the best Soviet novels are those which, like *The Quiet Don*, are least didactic. The Soviet novel also suffers from writers' unwillingness, backed by official policy, to undertake technical experiment. Above all, the Soviet novelist is unable to give a picture of the world as it appears to him, unless he indeed happens to be a strong supporter of official theories—in which case his picture of the world will have nothing new to offer the reader.

Many of the great Russian novels of the classical period are the work of eccentric thinkers like Dostoyevsky and Tolstoy, whose views few readers would dream of sharing. Yet to look at the world through the eyes of a Tolstoy or Dostoyevsky is to have one's horizons extended and one's experience enriched, as the result of their immense literary talent. The study of Soviet literature is also an enriching experience, but it is very much less of a literary process. As has been indicated, some of the most valuable works as a subject for study are among the weakest from a literary point of view.

Soviet literature is a new phenomenon on the world stage and criticism has not yet built the tools to deal with it adequately—for which very reason it is an absorbing and stimulating study. Meanwhile the Russian novel, as an aesthetic experience, is by no means dead, but it is a sad commentary on Soviet conditions that the only great Russian novel to have appeared since *The Quiet Don* is a banned work —Pasternak's *Doctor Zhivago*. Perhaps the merits of this have been exaggerated in the West—it is an immensely moving and important work, but less impressive as an example of the novelist's craft. However, until Soviet writers are permitted to purvey a personal vision of the world, unhampered by the thought of officials breathing down their necks, Pasternak's masterpiece is likely to remain unrivalled.

The Novel Today

Some of the finest exponents of the art of the novel

C P SNOW · PAMELA HANSFORD JOHNSON

ERIC LINKLATER · MURIEL SPARK

JOHN WAIN · JANE DUNCAN · RUMER GODDEN

CHARLES MORGAN · WALTER MACKEN · PAUL HORGAN

MARGARET KENNEDY · STORM JAMESON

are published by **Macmillan**

Today, *as for over one hundred years,*
Macmillan take great pride in their fiction list
New writers are always welcome

Macmillan
St Martin's Street London WC2

UNIVERSITY OF EDINBURGH

At no time in our history has the need for higher education been greater : at no time has the demand been more insistent, or the requirements more exacting. The scope and content of many aspects of scientific learning has more than doubled in the course of a generation ; and with the growth of science, a corresponding efficacy in the processes of general and humane education has become essential.

The University of Edinburgh, conscious of the immensity and responsibility of its task, is painfully aware that its physical assets, in the shape of laboratories, classrooms, ancillary accommodation, and the necessary equipment, are inadequate and out of date.

These things cost money. Though much will be provided from Government sources, the University itself will have to meet the cost of a substantial part of its building programme, which, over the next few years, will involve the expenditure of many millions of pounds. To this end it is making an Appeal to all its graduates and friends, and has already raised more than £363,000. Still more is required if our young men and women are to have the education they desire and deserve.

All contributions will be most gratefully acknowledged, and full information on the University's needs and plans, with advice on methods of contributing, will gladly be sent on application to the Secretary to the University, Old College, South Bridge, Edinburgh 8.

A PUBLISHER IS KNOWN
BY THE COMPANY HE KEEPS

is the title of a film prepared by Louis de Rochemont Associates which is to be shown at the Edinburgh Film Festival. Directed by Jules Victor Schwerin, it is principally made up of cinematic sequences showing some of the authors published by Alfred A. Knopf who were photographed by him during the Twenties and Thirties. They include:—

Thomas Mann   Walter de la Mare   Oswald Spengler

H. L. Mencken   Max Beerbohm   Willa Cather   Maurice Baring

Sigrid Undset   George Jean Nathan   Logan Clendening

Kahlil Gibran   Elinor Wylie   Carl Van Vechten

Witter Bynner   Warwick Deeping   Emma Goldman

Joseph Hergesheimer   Ernest Newman

Mr. Knopf relates on the accompanying sound-track the circumstances under which the films were made and something about his subjects. An unusually large number of their works continues to be available over the imprint of

ALFRED · A · KNOPF, Publisher

american fiction since the second world war

by MICHAEL MILLGATE

Michael Millgate is Lecturer in English at the University of Leeds. He is the author of 'William Faulkner' in Oliver and Boyd's Writers and Critics series.

Any account of American fiction since the Second World War must necessarily open with the names of writers who had already made a reputation for themselves before the war began. One thinks, for example, of the novelists who first became known in the nineteen-twenties—Sinclair Lewis, John Dos Passos, Ernest Hemingway, and William Faulkner —and of those who established themselves a little later— John Steinbeck, Robert Penn Warren, James Gould Cozzens, John O'Hara, and even Carson McCullers, who published her first novel as early as 1940. With few exceptions, however, these older novelists have not done their finest work in this post-war period. Carson McCullers, with *Member of the Wedding* (1946) and *The Ballad of the Sad Café* (1951), is certainly one exception, Cozzens is another —though his best novel is *Guard of Honor* (1948), not the more famous *By Love Possessed* (1957)—and, fine though

Night Rider (1939) undoubtedly is, most critics have felt that Penn Warren is at his best in *All the King's Men* (1946). Sinclair Lewis, on the other hand, added little to his reputation with the novels he published between 1945 and his death in 1951; the weakness of Dos Passos's recent books has led to an unjustified neglect of his very distinguished novels of the 'twenties and 'thirties; Steinbeck appears to have lost his way in whimsicality; and O'Hara's work, for all its amplitude of social documentation, has come to seem increasingly repetitious.

The most interesting cases, of course, and the most important, are those of Hemingway and Faulkner. There has been much praise and much criticism of *The Old Man and the Sea* (1952), the highly symbolistic short novel about a Caribbean shark-fisherman which was the last book Hemingway published before his death in 1961, but the reception of the earlier *Across the River and Into the Trees* (1950) was almost uniformly hostile. Indeed, unless the appearance of posthumously published material produces a major critical reappraisal, there now seems to be fairly general agreement both that Hemingway's achievement has been somewhat overestimated and that his best work dates from the nineteen-twenties. But if the pendulum of critical esteem has begun to swing away from Hemingway, as was to be expected in the years immediately following his death, it has only just finished swinging towards William Faulkner. In 1945 none of Faulkner's books was in print in America, now he is widely acknowledged as one of the greatest writers of modern American, and perhaps world, literature. This reputation, it must be said, rests primarily on such books as *The Sound and the Fury* (1929), *As I Lay Dying* (1930), *Light in August* (1932), and *Absalom, Absalom!* (1936): Faulkner's novels since 1945—*Intruder in the Dust* (1948), *Requiem for a Nun* (1951), *A Fable* (1954), *The Town* (1957), and *The Mansion* (1959)—have lacked the power of his greatest work and have often tended to be patterned in accordance with the preconceived necessities of some moral or social statement. They state too explicitly the values which the earlier books implicitly embodied and enacted. Even so, his last books, *The Mansion* and *The Reivers*, contain some excellent writing, and one must admire and pay tribute to the remarkable way in which Faulkner, after the war, set about reconstituting himself as a novelist upon a radically different basis.

When one turns to the younger novelists who have made their appearance in the post-war period, the picture becomes at once more crowded and more confused. The period has not, perhaps, been one of the greatest American fiction has known—it is clearly not so great as the middle of the last century, for example, or as the 'twenties and early 'thirties of this—but it has been one of remarkable variety and vitality. It is the number of notable names that strikes one, rather than the inescapability of one or two outstanding figures, and in such a period, and at such close range, it is difficult to seize upon the novels and novelists most likely to achieve permanent importance.

One general point that can be made is the extent to which novelists of very different abilities and ambitions have been drawn to the treatment of similar areas of society and the exploration of similar political, social, and moral issues. The immediate post-war years, naturally enough, saw the publication of a great many novels about the war itself and about military organisations: the most important of these were Cozzens's *Guard of Honor*, James Jones's *From Here to Eternity* (1951), and Norman Mailer's *The Naked and the Dead* (1948), a powerful book remarkable both for its vivid impressions of warfare in the Pacific and for its angry portrayal of the army as a power-structure, destructive of the individual and inherently fascistic. More recently, there has been a series of novels about universities and academic life, notably Mary McCarthy's brilliantly satirical *The Groves of Academe* (1952), still the outstanding book of its kind, Randall Jarrell's *Pictures from an Institution* (1954), Vladimir Nabokov's *Pnin* (1957), and Howard Nemerov's *The Homecoming Game* (1957). There has also been a whole flood of more crudely 'sociological' fiction, much of it with an exposé angle, about big business, unions, governmental bureaucracy, advertising, Hollywood, television and radio, professional boxing, and so on; J. P. Marquand (who died in 1960), John Brooks, Budd Schulberg, and one or two others have brought a degree of distinction to this type of fiction,

but most of it is of a sub-literary kind. What the 'military' and 'academic' novels, and the best of the other 'sociological' novels, have in common is a central concern with one of the dominating phenomena of modern American society, the growth of vast bureaucratic organisations in every area of the national life, from armies to universities, from business corporations to hospitals.

If some of these books about the individual in relation to the organisation have inevitably and deliberately tended to be claustrophobic in effect, other recent novels have tended in a quite opposite direction, bringing into modern American fiction almost for the first time something of the spirit of the picaresque, together with a feeling for the land itself in all its vastness and variety. This is one of the most notable qualities of Nabokov's *Lolita* (1958), though the novel's vein is satirical, and it is one of the few really attractive features of Jack Kerouac's *On the Road* (1957). J. D. Salinger's *The Catcher in the Rye* (1951) and Ralph Ellison's *Invisible Man* (1952), in their very different ways, also have something of this feeling, but the novelist who most consistently seeks and achieves the richness and amplitude of the picaresque is Saul Bellow, undoubtedly one of the most important novelists to have emerged since the war. Three of his books, *Dangling Man* (1944), *The Victim* (1947), and *Seize the Day* (1956) are short, carefully-wrought studies, but his most recent work, *Henderson the Rain King* (1959), returns to the expansive, immensely vigorous, picaresque mode of *The Adventures of Augie March* (1953). Henderson, the restless, ageing American millionaire, is engaged in the search for personal identity and significance—as are all of Bellow's heroes to a greater or lesser degree. The story is told by Henderson himself, and the energy of the man is powerfully expressed in the forceful, flexible prose that is based on the spoken voice yet is capable of rising above it, in a natural transition, to exuberant, poetic outbursts of agony and joy.

One of Bellow's greatest achievements, then, is his style, but the supreme stylist of post-war American fiction is J. D. Salinger. The great distinction of his first novel, *The Catcher in the Rye*, is the brilliance of the writing, the precisely sensitive evocation of the speech of a sixteen-year-old

American boy at a particular moment in time; but its great success has derived not only from the sheer seduction of the style but also from the presentation of the yearnings and frustrations of those, adults as well as adolescents, who live in modern over-organised societies. Salinger's second novel, *Franny and Zooey* (1961), has the same stylistic felicity as the earlier book, so that the characters become vividly alive simply through the dialogue, but the material of the book, what the characters talk about, has a curious aridity, a willed and arbitrary quality, which prevents it from setting up in its readers the kind of reverberations that were produced by *The Catcher in the Rye*. Salinger is also a master of a certain kind of short story—indeed, *Franny and Zooey* is perhaps more accurately described not as a novel but as two short stories—and in this respect his name is often associated with that of other contributors to the *New Yorker* magazine. Mary McCarthy belongs partly to this group—see, for example, her short story collections *The Company She Keeps* (1943) and *Cast a Cold Eye* (1950)—but of recent years, and particularly since the publication of her novel *A Charmed Life* (1955), she has turned increasingly to such non-fictional forms as theatre criticism, travel writing, and autobiography. Also associated with the *New Yorker*, though they have little in common save stylistic brilliance, are J. F. Powers, an outstanding short-story writer whose first novel is due to appear shortly, and John Updike, who has been highly praised both for his short stories and for his novels. His *Rabbit, Run* (1960) was especially well received and he is widely considered to be, along with George P. Elliott and John Barth, among the most promising of the younger American novelists.

Another group of writers which has contributed a great deal to American fiction since the Second World War is that sometimes loosely referred to as the 'Southern school'—although these writers do not, any more than the 'New Yorker group', form anything nearly so coherent as a 'school'. Katherine Anne Porter and Eudora Welty are still writing, of course, as well as William Faulkner, Robert Penn Warren and Carson McCullers, and several new writers have appeared, notably Truman Capote, who has, however, become increasingly absorbed into the New York milieu, Flannery O'Connor, a writer of intense and terrifying short stories who has not yet written a wholly successful novel, and William Styron. *Lie Down in Darkness* (1951), Styron's first book, is a long, dense, carefully-structured, somewhat ornate novel set in Virginia, *The Long March* (1952) is a brilliant short novel about a Marine training exercise, while his most recent book, *Set This House on Fire* (1960), set mainly in Italy, returns to the scale and to something like the manner of *Lie Down in Darkness*. Styron is one of the most impressive of contemporary American novelists and the only one, with the possible exception of Bellow, who seems able to create within the bounds of a single novel a comprehensive, minutely concrete and wholly convincing fictional world.

There remain many novelists whom it has not been possible to discuss in a brief impressionistic survey of this kind: one thinks, for example, of Nelson Algren, James Baldwin, James Purdy, and especially of Wright Morris and Bernard Malamud, two figures who are obviously important but who do not fit readily into any convenient category—except in so far as Morris can be characterised as a midwestern writer and Malamud linked with Bellow and others in a group of Jewish novelists. Too many other writers, of course, have received only the casual injustice of a passing mention; but one writer whom it seems impossible merely to mention in passing, in the context of the 'military' novel, is Norman Mailer, an isolated, intransigent, unassimilable figure on the contemporary literary scene. He has published only three novels—*The Naked and the Dead*, *Barbary Shore* (1951), and *The Deer Park* (1955)—and only the first of them can be judged a success, yet his work is always alive, always explorative, always intelligent, always demanding attention. His recent collection of essays, stories, and extracts, *Advertisements for Myself* (1959), and notably the piece entitled 'The Time of her Time' (omitted from the English edition of the book), is only the latest indication that he may one day publish something that will establish him once and for all in the first rank of post-war American novelists alongside Bellow, Salinger, and Styron.

west indian novels

by KARINA WILLIAMSON

Karina Williamson has taught at the Universities of Edinburgh and Upsala, and at Newbattle Abbey College.

The West Indian novel is still a very young growth. It scarcely existed before 1950, when the publication of V. S. Reid's first novel, *New Day*, and Edgar Mittelholzer's second, *A Morning at the Office*, seemed to inaugurate a period of intense activity which so far has produced nearly fifty novels, the work of more than a dozen writers: Reid, Roger Mais, John Hearne, Andrew Salkey, Neville Dawes, Namba Roy, and Fitzroy Fraser, from Jamaica; Samuel Selvon and V. S. Naipaul from Trinidad; George Lamming and Geoffrey Drayton from Barbados; Mittelholzer, Lauchmonen, Jan Carew and Wilson Harris from British Guiana.

Most of these writers are young, not yet out of their thirties, but the novels themselves bear few marks of juvenility. They have the assurance, the purposefulness and command of technique that are usually associated with a mature tradition. The explanation of this precocity might seem to be that West Indian writers have had the veteran stock of the English novel to draw on. But in fact, when every allowance has been made for the skills and techniques they inherited, it must be said that the West Indian novel has grown up more in opposition to the parent tradition than in its footsteps, and indeed rebellion against what is often felt as the dead weight of an alien culture has itself been a stimulus towards the development of a distinctively West Indian tradition of writing.

For a West Indian writer with roots in Africa or India is in a curious position. He is cut off from the traditions of his own race, yet does not feel fully heir to the traditions of Europe that are imposed on him from his schooldays. Lamming likens his plight to that of the American negro who feels, in James Baldwin's phrase, 'a kind of bastard of the West'; but while American negroes have developed a sense of kinship through race, the peculiar nature of ethnic groupings in the West Indies has prevented any general development of this kind. Add to this the diverse and scattered character of the West Indian territories, and it seems a miracle that any sense of shared experience or common cultural aims should emerge at all. That it has is due largely to the two features of their history which have been most crucial in their social and economic development: slavery and colonialism. Whatever its ties with English traditions, the West Indian novel exists as a distinctive form because it reflects the consciousness of a people whose society has been shaped, above all, by these two pressures.

Not that all the novels aim at a diagnosis of the state of West Indian society. Some, such as Selvon's *A Brighter Sun* and its sequel, *Turn Again Tiger*, or Naipaul's *Miguel Street*, have won modest but assured success by recording with fidelity, humour and compassion the quality of everyday life. In others—Mittelholzer and Hearne provide examples —the story is modified, but not determined by its West Indian setting.

At the other extreme, the writer's consciousness of the forces that have shaped his society finds direct expression through historical fiction, as in Reid's *New Day*, a family saga depicting the progress in Jamaica from slavery towards self-government, and Namba Roy's *Black Albino*, set in the eighteenth century among the Maroons, runaway slaves who established their own enclaves in the Jamaican highlands and eventually won themselves a measure of autonomy. Roy has lapses into didacticism, the occupational hazard of

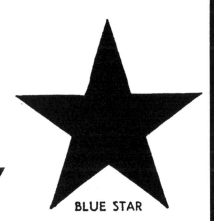

historical writing aggravated by the fact that, like all West Indian novelists, he is writing for the foreign reader. For the cultural dependence of the West Indies on England has fostered a feeling of contempt among educated West Indians for the homegrown product. The situation is changing; so much, indeed, that the cult of West Indian arts is itself satirised in John Figueroa's short story, 'Ars Longa; Vita Brevis'. But there are practical reasons why West Indian writers must still rely on foreign readers for their livelihood, and two weaknesses in West Indian writing, the tendency to proselytise and to exploit national idiosyncrasies for easy returns, can be traced to this cause.

Where Reid and Roy leave off, Lamming, Selvon, and Dawes take up the theme, showing in different ways the continuing pressure of the past on the present. 'You mus' never forget, after all your education, that your grandfather was a slave', says the hero's father in Dawes's novel, *The Last Enchantment*, and the dependence of privilege on colour which is the evil fruit of slavery is a major preoccupation of the book. Selvon's hope in *An Island is a World* seems to be that out of the débris of the past a new form of nationalism, tolerant and cosmopolitan, may be forged; but from the start West Indian solidarity was threatened, and has since been disrupted, by conflicting allegiances—to individual islands, to race—and it is the tension arising from these conflicts that gives the book its moments of power. Selvon is best, however, when he is least doctrinaire, as in his less ambitious novel, *The Lonely Londoners*, which conveys with force and immediacy the colonial's sense of rootlessness in his 'mother-country'. The use of dialect for both narrative and dialogue ('Is English we speaking' says a character with truth—English marvellously rejuvenated) not only gives a greater flexibility to Selvon's prose but also seems to liberate resources of feeling that are half stifled in *An Island is a World*.

The fullest analysis of the West Indian situation comes from Lamming's novels, particularly *In the Castle of my Skin* and *Of Age and Innocence*. Through the characters of the old negro Pa, of slave stock, and the landowner Creighton, re-presenting the dying white aristocracy, Lamming demonstrates movingly his thesis, that for master and slave alike, 'to be colonial is to be in a state of exile'. This idea of colonialism as alienation—from homeland and customs, traditional culture and values—is crystallised in Pa's dream, a passage of great beauty and power, in which ancestral memories stir and well up in the old man's mind. But a brief summary cannot do justice to the richness and complexity of Lamming's exploration of his theme through past and present in these two books. The urgency of his concern has wrenched the very form of the novel and he takes the poet's licence to speak through parable and symbolism: in his early days, he has said, 'prose always struck me as an inferior way for any serious writer to use words' and his favourite novelists were Conrad and Hardy. This eagerness to extend the resources of the novel, seen also, for example, in the use of dramatic devices in Mais's novels and myth and symbol in Wilson Harris's *Palace of the Peacock*, is one of the most promising features of West Indian novel writing.

It is clear from these novels that involvement with West Indian concerns gives prominence to certain themes, and the persistence of these themes in novels committed less openly, if at all, to specifically West Indian problems makes it possible to speak so confidently of 'the West Indian novel'. Thus conflicting national loyalties figure again in Mittelholzer's *Latticed Echoes*, which is mainly concerned with personal relationships. Drayton's *Christopher*, a subtle and arresting study of a child's development, also contains a tacit judgment on the values of the plantocracy; the same topic, viewed with more nostalgia than criticism, gives an extra dimension to John Hearne's novel, *The Faces of Love*, and the colour issue is at the centre of his *Voices under the Window*; *The Leopard*, in which Reid, with astonishing virtuosity, enters into the personality of a Kikuyu warrior, also dramatises the kind of clash of moralities—pagan and Christian, native and imposed—that is the point of two episodes from *In the Castle of my Skin*.

Especially conspicuous are ideas to do with identity,

Something to write home about!

LOOK OUT for this motorized bank –
one of several mobile offices of the
National Commercial Bank which serve
the more isolated parts of Scotland. We
pioneered the idea, and this may be your
unique chance of seeing a bank on the
move or even climbing a hill!
All our branches are at the service
of visitors to Scotland for cashing
Travellers' Cheques or changing
foreign currency.

National Commercial Bank of Scotland Limited

Banking service throughout Scotland and the world

self-respect, and integrity which, though not the preserve of West Indians, have particular relevance to their situation. The quest for identity and self-respect gives a strong undercurrent of pathos to Naipaul's latest and most impressive novel, *A House for Mr Biswas*. From time to time the smooth patina of Naipaul's narrative cracks and we are shown a glimpse of the vacuity and desolation that always threaten the hero, 'a blankness, a void like those in dreams, into which, past tomorrow and next week and next year, he was falling'. Naipaul and Lamming are antipathetic as writers, but as West Indians they share this sense of the precariousness of individuality. Higgins and Dickson in *The Emigrants* cling, like Mr Biswas, to external proofs of identity: status, training, a house, a job. The threat to identity is not always clearly formulated. For Biswas it is poverty on the one hand and domination by his Tulsi in-laws on the other; but his fears are the more powerful because they seem to be rooted in some deeper sense of inadequacy. Often—and here the West Indians are on common ground with writers all over the world—the Establishment is the threat, and integrity depends on the refusal to sell out, to conform to the standards of the masters: especially, to become Europeanised. This kind of betrayal figures, in different forms, in many novels. It is treated satirically by Fraser in *Wounds in the Flesh* and Naipaul in *The Mystic Masseur*. Naipaul's handling is subtle as well as funny, and the shock of his ending steals nothing from the perfection of its logic. Ganesh, the Hindu hero, rises from obscurity to fame and prosperity by exploiting his supposed gifts as a sage and mystic. The narrator, now in England, meets him after a gap of time:

'Pundit Ganesh!' I cried, running towards him. 'Pundit Ganesh Ramsumair!'

'G. Ramsey Muir', he said coldly.

Ramsay, the hero of *The Last Enchantment*, views the rewards of conformism won by his friend Hanson with a mixture of irony and envy—the dual pull is finely conveyed. But there is no ambivalence in the attitudes of Lamming and Mais; in fact it is Surjue's refusal, in *The Hills were Joyful together*, to surrender his integrity for any threat or inducement that gives him tragic stature. This, however, is only one thread in a novel which as a whole is a formidable indictment of urban society in Jamaica, a society which is shown to foster squalor and violence, the opportunist and the parasite, and make compassion and integrity futile. Beyond this determinist view of morality there is a broader fatalism, a recognition of the cosmic condition voiced in passing by an old market woman: 'Night fall so soon, you take two turns round the market square with your vegetable barrow, tired, siddung, shet you' eye, open it, Lawd, sun gone down.' The impressive gifts shown in Mais's three novels— his mythopoeic power, his humane but uncompromising morality, his inventiveness in structure and style, his insight into sub-rational levels of feeling where religion, superstition, and occultism merge into mania—show that his early death meant the loss of a major writer.

It is of course impossible to predict the way ahead for the West Indian novel, but it is also impossible to read far without a sense of excitement at the prospect of new areas of experience now opened up and latent resources of form and language which the experiments of Lamming, Mais, Harris, and others have only begun to draw on.

NATIONAL LIBRARY OF SCOTLAND

'English Literature'

an exhibition of MSS and of first and other early editions from the Library's own collection

---

OPEN DURING THE FESTIVAL: MONDAY TO SATURDAY 9.30 AM- 8.30 PM; SUNDAY 2 PM - 5 PM

THE EXHIBITION WILL REMAIN OPEN DURING NORMAL HOURS TILL 30TH SEPTEMBER

GEORGE IV BRIDGE, EDINBURGH

126

127

index to advertisers

George Allen and Unwin Ltd page 120
Bauermeister Booksellers page 44
Anthony Blond Ltd page 34
John Calder (Publishers) Ltd pages 58 and 59
Cassell page 30
Chatto & Windus and The Hogarth Press page 98
Constable page 127
Andre Deutsch page 102
K. D. Duval page 110
Edinburgh University Press page 2
Encounter page 20
Evergreen Books Ltd page 120
Eyre & Spottiswoode page 12
Faber and Faber Limited page 106
John Grant Booksellers Ltd page 26
Hamish Hamilton page 110
Harcourt, Brace & World, Inc. page 128
Heinemann page 10
Houghton Mifflin Company page 82
Michael Joseph Ltd page 16
Alfred A. Knopf page 116
William Maclellan page 105
Macmillan London page 114
Macmillan New York page 40
Methuen & Co Ltd page 54
National Commercial Bank of Scotland Ltd page 124
National Library of Scotland page 126
Nelson page 86
New Saltire page 127
Oliver & Boyd page 1
Olympia Press page 48
Oxford University Press page 38
The Paperback page 22
Penguin Books page 53
The Scotsman page 6
Scottish & Newcastle Breweries Ltd page 122
Secker & Warburg page 50
South of Scotland Electricity Board page 127
The University of Edinburgh page 115
The University Presses of Chicago, Columbia, Yale page 20
Weidenfeld & Nicolson page 97

*The Edinburgh Festival Society would like to thank the advertisers listed
above for making the production of 'The Novel Today' possible. They would
also like to acknowledge the generous assistance of all the publishers
and others who have given the Conference their support.*

Publishers of
Distinguished
Books

━━━━━━

Harcourt, Brace & World, Inc.
NEW YORK

Longmans Canada Limited
TORONTO

Rupert Hart-Davis
LONDON